Andrew C. Sparkes & Martti Silvennoinen (eds.)

Talking
BODIES

SoPhi

University of Jyväskylä 1999

GV
706
.4
T35.

SoPhi

University of Jyväskylä 1999

SoPhi publishes social sciences at the University of Jyväskylä, Finland, and it is located at the Department of Social Sciences and Philosophy. It provides a forum for innovative studies in social policy, sociology, political science and philosophy. SoPhi publishes 10–15 titles per year, both in Finnish and in English. Manuscripts are selected for publication on the basis of expert opinion.

Correspondence should be sent to publications editor Juha Virkki, Department of Social Sciences and Philosophy/Publications, University of Jyväskylä, P.O. Box 35, FIN-40351 Jyväskylä, Finland, tel. +358-(0)14-603123, fax +358-(0)14-603101, e-mail jutavi@dodo.jyu.fi.

Publications can be ordered from Kampus Kirja, Kauppakatu 9, FIN-40100 Jyväskylä, Finland (tel. +358-(0)14-603157, fax +358-(0)14-611143, e-mail kampuskirja@co.jyu.fi.

Visit SoPhi home page at http://www.jyu.fi/~yhtfil/sophi/sop.html

ISBN 951-39-0424-5

ISSN 1238-8025

Printed at Jyväskylä University Printing House, Jyväskylä 1999

Cover printed at ER-Paino, Laukaa 1999

Cover Tuija Tarkiainen

Layout Juha Virkki

CONTENTS

EXTREMITIES

METAMORPHOSES

TO THE READER

Sport has been one of the traditional stages for displaying the male body. For many men, becoming an athlete can be a crucial masculinizing experience, engendering a self-confidence that generalizes to all aspects of their life. In a similar fashion Robert Connell (1995, 54) argues, "In historically recent times, sport has come to be the leading definer of masculinity in mass culture. Sport provides a continuous display of men's bodies in motion."

However, not all men enjoy the experience of playing sport. As Ian Harris (1995, 124) points out. "Competitive sports can be painful for those men who feel inferior because they cannot perform to the standards expected of them. For other men who do not succeed, the sportsman message can cause them to doubt their worth as men." Furthermore, as Connell (1995, 54) suggests, "The constitution of masculinity through bodily performance means that gender is vulnerable when the performance cannot be sustained – for instance, as a result of physical disability."

Michael Quinn Patton writes in his book *Qualitative Evaluation and Research Methods* (1990, 7,143) as follows: "There is no burden of proof. There is only the world to experience and understand. Shed the burden of proof to lighten the load for the journey of experience (...) When in doubt, observe and ask questions. When certain, observe at length, and ask many more questions."

This is a book of nothing but stories. The narrators are white academic men who have become members of the middle class and who live in Western consumer culture, and one woman. We can only con-

5

jecture what kind of narratives we might hear from other people from other parts of the world. The warp thread running through the stories collected here is, in one way or another, the male body and male identity; manifested as transformations and crises. You, as a reader, may notice that many of the stories are embodied and told as 'flashbulb' memories, which are firmly fixed in a certain time and place. You may also find some of the tales daringly intimate. They do, after all, tell about people under their real names. Each of the writers has taken this ethically important question into consideration.

Talking Bodies becomes an attempt to fill in some noticeable gaps in mainstream gender studies and sports sociology by focusing directly upon the subjective experiences of men, their multiple senses of self and shifting identities, the relationships they form with their bodies, and, over time with the bodies of other people in their environment. It does this by pulling together a variety of narratives about men's embodied experiences of sport, and about the construction of specific masculine senses of self. These male stories approach also the question of the body that is transformed in a process where a reliable, controlled, obedient and harmless body becomes, rapidly or slowly, a troublesome, disruptive, indefinite and even an anguished body.

There are some cogent reasons explaining why we have brought this book to be edited in Finland, especially in Jyväskylä. There is something of a tradition of narrative and autobiographical studies here. In 1994 *International Review for the Sociology of Sport* published a special issue on the 'Finnish School', as the editor Henning Eichberg (...) called a group of people who had put aside a 'hardcore' empiricism, each of them in their own way. In the following year Department of Social Policy, University of Jyväskylä collected a report on *Strangers in Sport* (Veijola et al. 1995), which was a mixture of the theoretical and the personal. The third thread goes back to 1997, when the Publishing Unit of the Jyväskylä University Library brought out a book, *Härkätaistelija kentän reunalla. Kertomuksia isistä, lapsista ja urheilusta* (A bullfighter on the edge of the arena. Stories about fathers, sons and sport) (Silvennoinen et al. 1997). Three authors (Innanen, Sparkes and Silvennoinen) now contributing to *Talking Bodies* also wrote each a chapter for *Härkätaistelija*.

We hope that the finished book is a collection of texts which will appeal to a wide audience, from the lay reader to undergraduate and postgraduate students, as well as to teachers in the fields of gender studies, exercise and sport sciences and the sociology and psychology of the body and embodiment.

* * *

The book is divided into four sections (see the contents of the book). *Mark Sudwell* starts the collection off with his text "The Body Bridge", exploring one dimension of the ever-changing relationship between father and son. It takes the form of a story written in two parts, tracing the past history of his relationship with his father from earliest childhood memories to the present day, to a time when the boy begins to see and feel the mortality of his father, and with that mortality a sense of normality.

Jim Denison has written two texts. "Boxed In" uses a narrative self to show how a competitive athlete feels when he suffers an injury that jeopardizes his career. The second one, "Men's Selves and Sport", is based on interviews with retired sportsmen. Denison has used their stories in an attempt to convey what he considers the key moments in his own and in his subjects' lives and discuss the ways in which the development of positive identities beyond sport becomes problematic.

Peter Swan's "Three Ages of Changing" is a short story about the world that opens in changing rooms. In this chapter Swan portrays his own identity as a performer, teacher and observer – describing how the changing-room world is masculine, jokified and both enabling and constraining for the boys.

In different parts of the book *David Jackson* gives us four poems which explore his personal experiences of the connections between sport, bodies and masculinities. He says: "I've got back to writing poems after years of writing more analytically. This has been a refreshing shift for me allowing me to explore areas like my war-time boyhood, growing up as a boy, schooling, manly bodies and the problems of not having one, hairiness, sport, masculine sexualities, dreams, fantasies."

Andrew Sparkes demonstrates how to explore the reflexive relationship between the body and the self over time in ways that fuse the personal and the societal. In his text "The Fragile Body-Self" he reveals his emotional dimensions and the consequences of an interrupted body project: "Who did I think I was, who do I think I am and who do I think I might be in the future?" The narrative focuses upon himself as a middle-aged, white, heterosexual, middle-class male, and a 'failed body' and upon memories of an elite, performing, working-class body that housed a 'fatal flaw'.

Martti Silvennoinen has written two chapters. "Anguish of the Body" is a short story about two male childhood experiences where a wounded body becomes temporarily the only 'punctum' of life. His second chapter, "My Body as a Metaphor", reveals three personally important memory traces which, as the author puts it, have shaped his adult life as a man doing research.

Andrew Sparkes and *Brett Smith* draw upon life-history data to focus on the identity dilemmas of a small group of men who have suffered spinal cord injury while playing rugby football and now define themselves as disabled. Their words illustrate how the body-self relationship has shifted from an absent presence to something that is 'other', problematic and alien.

David Brown interprets "The Social Meaning of Muscle". This chapter examines the embodied experiences of becoming, and of being. He says: "Drawing upon life history interviews, male bodybuilders are shown to inhabit a loosely hierarchical subworld. But, on the other hand, countering the view of bodybuilders being locked mechanistically into systems of surveillance that produce docile bodies, their life history narratives show how their bodies under construction provide potential sites of self-transformation and identity reconstruction."

Mikko Innanen reads and rethinks the diary that he kept for about a year in 1996. Recently separated from his common-law wife, he travelled to a kibbutz in Israel to escape a life that had become intolerable. "Secret Life in the Culture of Thinness" is a story about male anorexia. It is an attempt to understand the links between the break in his identity, the interruption of a male body project.

Douglas Kleiber and *Susan Hutchinson* tell a 'Hero's Story'. What role does the hero's story play in a man's life after he becomes disabled? The men's stories discussed in this chapter are not taken to be real pictures of their lives. Rather, what they symbolize as stories of heroes the way in which the altered self is transformed into the hero of one's reconstructed life story – for these men, for the people they live with d receive treatment from, and to our culture more generally.

Our thanks go to the authors, to Eeva Jokinen for reading the manuscript and providing many valuable comments, to Hannu Hiilos for translating the Finnish texts, to Donald Adamson for helping us to choice the poems, to LIKES Research Center for the financial aid – and to SoPhi for publishing our book.

In Jyväskylä and Exeter, March 1999

Andrew C. Sparkes   *Martti Silvennoinen*

References

Connell, R.W. (1995) *Masculinities*. Cambridge: Polity Press.

Eichberg, H. (1994) The Narrative, the Situational, the Biographical. Scandinavian Sociology of Body Culture traying a third Way. *International Review for the Sociology of Sport* (29) 1, 99-12.

Harris, I. (1995) *Messages Men Hear. Constructing Masculinities*. London: Taylor & Francis.

Veijola, S.; Bale, J. & Sironen, E. (1995) (Eds.) *Strangers in Sport. Reading Classics of Social Thought*. Department of Social Policy. Working Papers 91. University of Jyväskylä.

Patton, Q. M. (1990) *Qualitative Evaluation and Research Methods*. Newbury Park, CA: Sage.

THROUGH
SHARPENED
EYES

Mark Sudwell

THE BODY BRIDGE

The Making of A Body

My father: born in 1944, as an only child, he grew up in working class South London just after the war. As a young boy he had trained as a gymnast and springboard diver. By the age of eighteen he had won almost every London county competition at least once. In my grandmother's album there is an old black and white picture of him when he was twenty-ish, stood in his gymnast's vest, chalked hands, a handsome smile and a powerful physique with muscles tightly flexed. He stands amongst a pyramid of trophies and shinning silver cups – the bounty of his expertise. A modest couple still sit proudly in his lounge, below the collection of medals that hang in a frame above the fireplace. He was good.

In 1963 he moved to an elite, all male, Physical Education College in the South of England. In 1964 he was awarded a place in the Great Britain squad and competed at the World Student Games in Budapest. Soon after his return he developed tuberculosis (still very much a killer in the sixties) and retired from competitive sport. His tuberculosis cost him the scholarship he had been awarded to study at a major university in the United States. He eventually recovered from his illness, married, and became a teacher of Physical Education.

He hadn't actually planned it that way. As a youth he had restrained his academic ability quite successfully; so much so that after a poor performance in his 'A' levels his place at Loughborough Colleges was withdrawn. He got work as a telephone salesman; Christmas cards were his goods. His future looked, well, pretty uneventful really. It was at this moment that his skills as a gymnast would change the direction of his life: a chance meeting with one of his old coaches resulted in strings being pulled and a place at the PE college he attended. Quite simply, the fact that my dad was a bit tasty on a pommel horse is the thin thread that leads to my existence. Hours of training as a child brought him physical strength, balance, speed, and flexibility; that in turn brought him trophies and medals, a place at university, a teaching certificate on the wall, a job, a wife, two children and a house far the smog of London.

I, on the other hand, was fat. I remember very little about my child-hood that isn't directly related to this fact. I was also shy, extremely shy, a derivative of the fatness I presume. Fat, shy, and a worryingly slow learner. A child can't learn very much sitting in the corner alone; I was that child. At the age of eight my father had already started to collect trophies and, due to my grandmother's dream of him becoming a stage talent, studied dancing, singing, and the piano. At the same age I could barely read and write. My parents and teachers thought I might be dyslexic, after all I was from good genetic stock and my older sister was excelling in her studies. They were wrong, I was just plain stupid.

My sister just made things worse. Three years older, one of the bright-est in her peer group, the teachers praised her. She was musical and artistic like our father. She acted and, like our mother, was a talented dancer; winning regional acclaim. She was also a gymnast and an ath-lete. Everyone loved her, even me. She was our fairly tale Bo Peep, and I followed behind in my own distinctively sheepish manner. *As some-thing of an aside: I find my eye's are particularly sensitive to sun light — supposedly something to do with the blue pigment. However, when caught on a bright day without sunglasses I sometimes muse to myself that my constant squinting results from forever standing in my sister's shadow as a child.* It was all too much for the shy, fat boy. Unconsciously, I resigned myself from life.

What I remember being particularly good at was watching TV; I could watch that thing hour after hour. I'd even pretend to be ill so I could miss school, stay at home, and watch TV all day. I was a dab hand at faking a sudden fever: Just ignore all calls to get up, hold your breath and tense every muscle you can find. The result is a blotchy rash and a sweaty brow: perfect symptoms for a day off school. I hated school. School was a place where my brain hurt over the simplest of exercises, and Carl Webster would kick me until I begged for mercy (which I never did, but then I never kicked back either). And so it went on. For the first thirteen years of my life I slobbed my way towards being an overweight, over-spoilt, non-entity.

Why do I use the term non-entity? People tell me I'm being too severe. My mother tells me I was a very happy little boy, and I'm sure I was. But the 'me' now doesn't really remember the 'me' then; that's if there was a me back then for the me now to remember. I mean, I remember things, things that happened, things that we did, but it's as if these things didn't happen to me at all but someone else instead, as if I was just a spectator. I study a photograph of a young boy on his sixth or seventh birthday, surrounded by friends, all wearing paper pirates hats and brandishing cardboard cutlasses to run through anyone foolish enough to oppose them. And I remember sailing my dad's brown Ford Cortina down to the amusement arcade, and pirates plundering plastic money bags of two penny treasure. But I struggle to accept that I'm really the little boy in that photograph, sporting the biggest smile of all. It's as if we're two different people.

I remember the summer I learnt to swim. I guess I was about six. It was one of those seemingly endless summers that remain sheltered in our childhood; where youth colours the memories with burning sunshine, yellow lawns and days so long it was hard to stay awake to see daylight fade away into the shadows of evening. Every morning of that summer holiday we would ride out through the lanes to the holiday camp where my father worked in the evenings as part of the entertainment. The camp had a small open air swimming pool, with leaves and dirt, and a few insect corpses floating motionless in the corners. During the day it would heave with the lobster pink fleshy bodies of the camp site guests, but it was a little too cool for the holiday makers at this time of the morning; they much preferred to sleep in and let the midmorning sun do its work.

There we would swim. Well, my sister would swim, she could already. I, donned in armbands that were too big and an oversized diver's face mask (I hated water going up my nose) would simply float around, head under the water, kicking my feet only when I needed to pursue an old plaster or a piece of dirt that had been disturbed by my sister's splashing. My sister's swimming progressed quickly while I developed a strong capacity to hold my breath for long periods of time. No joke I'm afraid.

Looking back, I think I longed to be in my sister's place: achieving, being noticed. Not that I wasn't noticed, my parents were always very loving towards both of us. But I noticed my sister, whereas I didn't tend to notice myself too much. My father and I weren't close, or at least I don't recall feelings of that nature. I wanted so much to be nearer to him, like my sister, but there was a divide between us over which neither of us could reach.

I was about thirteen when my father asked me to accompany him to the gym where he had been training for a few weeks. He had been trying to strengthen the muscles that supported his sick spine, worn from years of over-use. It wasn't really a proper gym. It was a big, old garage with a couple of benches, some bars, dumbbells, and a few loose weights. A rickety leg machine sat in the corner, and a plastic jug of water always stood by the doorway. I remember the benches being cold to lie on in the winter, the bars sticking to my hands like ice cubes. And Ken, the owner, would stutter our names from under his bushy moustache as we arrived.

At first I'd not wanted to go; my father had tried before to get me interested in sport. When I was nine or ten he took me to his squash club and enrolled me in the junior league - my first match to be played that morning. I remember being pushed out into the cold, heavily walled court, my beautifully white PE kit gleaming under the bright lights (my PE kit had never been given a particularly hard time). My racket was heavy and, even though it was a child's size, my forearm soon began to ache from holding it. My opponent was another boy, same age as me but easily half my size; his stringy limbs dangled loosely from the openings of his T-shirt and shorts while I, well, I was more of a fleshy slick that oozed from any gap I could find.

Our father's stood together in the gallery watching with the others. The entire scene was like some fifties horror movie: 'Stick Thing meets The Blob'. It was useless. I was useless. Stick Thing's speed and agility, combined with the uncanny ability to actually hit the little green ball was just too much for the sluggish and uncoordinated Blob. I tried so hard, at least that's the way I remember it. I wanted to beat the other boy; if not for my sake then for my father's. I remember leaving the court and actually feeling sorry for my father, that he should have got me as a son rather than the other boy.

The gym was different. Perhaps it was because little physical skill was required, just effort. Perhaps it was the lack of a spying audience, eager to witness my inability. Or maybe it was because, even though I was carrying a few extra pounds, my entire family tree were mesomorphic, meaning: of a muscular build. Although I was out of condition, and tired very quickly, I was stronger than my father had anticipated. I could see he was pleased with my performance, possibly for the first time.

From then on we trained three nights a week, but more importantly, we talked; we talked of weight training and becoming strong at first, but we progressed. My father would talk of his youth, his parents (who I had never really known), and of life. We played squash at weekends. I hadn't improved since that terrible morning at the squash club but it didn't seem to matter. We had a lot of catching up to do. Sport gave my father a way of imparting all the things he knew to his son; we had found a frequency for communication. I distinctly remember receiving my first lesson in sex education as a result of asking my father, as we were showering after a game of squash, why he was always able to obtain what seemed a fantastic lather, thick and bubbly white, all over his body, while after I had rubbed my skin with the bar of soap nothing but a pathetic slippery, rather oily, translucent coating covered me. He calmly explained how the hairs on his body helped the soap to lather and that one day my body would be the same. Without either of us realising, our conversation simply wandered off from this point and, as we changed and made our way home, happily strolled through all those pastures of proclamation many parents and children fear to tread.

Something was happening to us but I was too busy studying him to notice.

It was during these evenings at the gym that I first got to know my father; to listen to him talk about himself and his beliefs. At that time I just enjoyed his company, his attention. My sister, at sixteen, was now more interested in parties and boyfriends. I still had no intrinsic desire for physical exercise, although I never told him that. I went because I started to feel like a son.

At the time I was unaware that my body was undergoing somewhat of a metamorphoses. For the next two years, and for all the training, my body feasted itself on the hormonal activity that accompanies this part of life. I grew up, but mainly I grew out. Training during the week with dad had been replaced by training after school for the rugby and basketball teams. Saturday was match day, and Sunday was squash with dad – I was even showing some improvement here. Other than that, I ate and slept whenever possible as my body lost its fat and replaced it with muscle. I was quickly becoming the body in the old black and white photo; smiling, flexing, trophy collecting.

I soon found myself as the captain of the school's rugby team. Off the field I was still pretty much the shy and retiring type. On the field I found a wonderful sense of freedom and confidence in my abilities. My body had always been a thing that brought nothing but embarrassment. That was to change.

We were a good side and rarely left the battle field in defeat. I had never won anything before in my life. My new body had brought me victory and it was a sweet, sweet feeling. The other boys in the team and in my school class now saw me as a valuable friend and I was quickly accepted into the higher echelons of my peer group, not stopping to look back at those 'squares' I had spent the previous years befriending. My new body had brought me a sense of camaraderie and respect from others. And that fateful day when Jason Baker pushed the old 'jelly belly' joke a little too far, resulting in his head and the classroom door colliding at high speed, the bullying stopped. I didn't notice at the time but my new body had given me power over others. I was no longer bullied. I had become the bully, and I liked it.

That year I started to play rugby for my local club's under 20's side. I was dwarfed by the smallest players, but my sister's boyfriend captained the side and, encouraged by my father, I went.

Playing for the Colts team was an important time for me. I gradually became recognised by the members of a team where I beard a closer resemblance to the mascot than a player. The other guys were all eighteen, nineteen, or twenty years old. To me they were nothing short of amazing. They were incredible athletes: huge bodies of muscle covered in fuzzy hair. They drove their own cars, they drank in the local pubs, they had sex with their girlfriends. Better than that, some had sex with other people's girlfriends and then laughed about it.

I was the baby of the team but I played hard. What I lacked in ability I made up for with dedication. I never missed a tackle – even if it meant being carried off the pitch to be sponged back to full consciousness - and I wouldn't stop running until the final whistle. I earned their respect and they taught me what they knew. I learnt quickly. I discovered beer, women, and I vomited in the street for the first time. Funny as it may seem, my father was proud. He even gave me a weekend tenner to spend after a Saturday game. And I still point out the post I clung too, while I first emptied my stomach contents on to the pavement, to friends when I visit home. That post is one of my trophies. No silver handles, or careful inscription, just a sign at the top saying: 'No parking at any time' (I guess it should've been: 'No puking ...').

That post is a trophy for, not just growing up, but for becoming someone. If I really had to pin it down, and even though since then I have changed in so many ways, I would say that I was born that night I stood in my parents hallway, my father standing in the doorway that led to the kitchen, my sister and Gareth, her boyfriend, near the front door, all of them waiting for me to reply. "Yes," I said, "I'll go." That same night I trained with the Colts for the first time. It rained so hard that thick muddy water ran from our hair and across our faces – every drop was illuminated in the fall of the floodlights – we did tackle practice, I got beat up, my body covered head to toe in black bruises. I was fifteen.

I guess that means I was conceived in a garage that was pretending to be a gym (and my mother wasn't even present – I hate to think what Freudians would think), and the two years in between must have been the gestation of my foetal personality, but I finally felt like a person. I had become a someone. Just as writers might look back fondly over the pages of their first short story, or scientists may remember carrying out their first experiment in their bedroom laboratories, I gently tap that post as I walk by and quietly relive those moments: the battle scars; the victories; the losses; the speed at which your breath is forced from your lungs as you are brought to the ground; the drunkenness; the Saturday night groupies; the coolness of wet mud on your face and the taste of it in your mouth; the Saturday night groupies; the feel of your eye's bulging from their sockets; the inverted view of the oncoming opposition pounding their way across the field to trample your flesh into the mud; and of course, the Saturday night groupies (being the baby of the team had its advantages). I remember all of these things with a warm smile.

My father was proud, so I was happy. Strangely enough, my father only once came to watch me play; something that has always intrigued me, but not enough to ask why. My new body had bridged the divide that had lay between us. We had found some common ground and built our relationship as father and son upon it. The father and his son. The master and his protégé. As I grew into an adult male I was delighted to find how physically alike I was to my father. I was the same height, the same build, we even sound the same. I remember finding an old picture of my father when he was nineteen or twenty, stood on the top of a diving board: it could have easily been a photo of me. For months I carried it around in my pocket, showing it to everyone I knew. I was everything he was.

The Unmaking

Dad sits in the arm chair in the lounge. His position is distinctively familiar: strangely upright and awkwardly rigid. His eye's glare into space. As I walk into the room they quickly move over to fix on me; the rest of his body remains quite still. I feel his stare and look away as I carefully walk over to the sofa and sit down; I really need to lie along the length of it but I know that will annoy him. I sit, and tell myself it's just a normal Sunday afternoon. Of course, it isn't. On a normal Sunday afternoon I would be able to lie around recovering from the night before, letting the smells of mum's roast dinner gently drift over me, bringing with them some sort of human consciousness.

I'm home from university for the holidays, as are my old school friends, hence the hangover.

Normally mum would have the radio on, singing along to her favourite old tunes while she peels bowl after bowl of vegetables. Normally dad would be in and out of the house: washing cars, revving engines, cutting grass, climbing ladders. "That's another job jobbed", he'd say, almost to himself, "What's next on the list then?" He's always been one for lists of jobs to be done my dad. Sometimes he'd sit down and read a paper, but only if every plug had been wired, every gutter cleared, and every hedge trimmed.

We sit there in a tense silence for a moment. I'm waiting for the inevitable; it's momentary.

"Decided to get up then," he says, his head still frozen in its place.

I breath out loudly; enough for him to hear it but too subtly for it to be clearly recognised as a sigh.

"Thought you were gonna lie in that shit pit all day."

I get up and go into the kitchen without saying anything. I know he can't follow me. And I know he's too proud to shout further remarks from that distance.

"Don't upset your father," mum whispers, "His back's playing him up."

I decide to stay in the kitchen and stir the gravy. If you don't want trouble it's best to stay out of trouble's way.

My father suffers from chronic back pain. The odds are most of you probably wouldn't even consider that a legitimate medical condition. We all get a bit of back ache right. Well mine is a different story. Mine is a story of pain; his pain, my mother's pain, mine and my sister's pain. Of course, I can only truly tell of my own, but no matter what anyone else thinks or says, I know that all of us shared the pain that haunts my father's body; we all got hurt.

When he has a flare up he's left in a great deal of pain, virtually immobile. He doesn't like to take his painkillers until he can no longer stand the pain – "gotta be man" and all that jazz – but by then it's too late; by then he's in such a shitty mood that the rest of us suffer with him. You see, he has a temper. I have it too – like father like son they say. It's like a bomb going off in your head when you don't get your own way. And that's what chronic back pain did to him; it took charge; it was in control.

Most of the time he's fine – which only adds to the problem – but he can no longer lift heavy objects. Hours of undue stress on his spine, all the twisting and bounding, has worn the vertebrae and left the joints of his spine weak. One wrong movement; one attempt at lifting something a little too heavy; one nights sleep in the wrong position, and those joints become inflamed; fluid gathering in the tissues around the joints, increasing the pressure, squeezing the nerves that emerge from his spine, strangling his very soul.

I guess those trophies were more expensive than he had first thought. The body that once stood proudly, flexing muscles behind all those trophies has gone now. The problem is the man remains. As he sits there, so still, it's like watching a trapped lion at the zoo. A man locked inside a corporeal cage. He lets out an unexpected roar at a passer by, sending them scurrying off to find safer places to be. His eye's shift restlessly around the room just as the lion repeatedly pads the length of his cell; both of them looking for an exit though they both know there is none. Bars of bone and gristle locked tight by a chain of swollen vertebrae. It's ironic that those parts of him that are the weakest have the strongest hold over this once great athlete.

Only the week before we had been on the squash court. Even here he is showing signs of decay. He is still infinitely better than I am but I'm nineteen years old. I'm strong, flexible, and fitter than I've ever been. Although it's obvious who's the better player, my speed and stamina allow me to chase his shots round the court. After thirty minutes he's one two games and I have none, but he's sweating and his breathing is heavy. I can always tell when he's tired. His shots become as clean, crisp and as deadly as he can make them. Not the shots he plays early on; the ones just inside my reach in an effort to prolong the rally and run me out. He can do it: I have more energy than he has shots. But by the third set he can't afford to let me return the ball and get a rally going; he needs this to be over as quickly as possible. We both leave the court exhausted.

I look at his naked body in the shower. He always used to seem so big and strong but now each part of him looks thin in comparison to mine – every part except the residue of fatty deposit that has, only recently, become noticeable around his waste. The tight wall of muscle that used to fortify his chest has sagged, and the hairs have become grey like those at the sides of his head. The ones on his head make him look sophisticated, elegant; these make him look old.

I've always struggled to think of him as becoming old – although nowadays time is letting my imagination off the hook by giving me a taste of the real thing. In a similar fashion, I could never imagine my father as a child; he was always too big, too strong, too much of my dad to be anything other than that. Children are small and weak; they don't know the answer to your every question and they can't walk up the stairs on their hands; how could he have possibly been one of those? No, not my dad.

I did end up going to university after all. I studied Sport Science. Why? Because it had 'sport' in the title of course. Dad had always tried to get me into teaching – the only thing he really knew I guess – but I felt I was destined for something bigger. I had only nearly missed the opportunity to fly in the Navy and I still had ambitions for such coolness. However, it was during my time at university that I started to notice a change. I couldn't tell if it was me, him, or both of us, but something was wrong and it scared me.

I went to university for two specific reasons: to play rugby and to work on my maths; that way I was virtually guaranteed a place for pilot training. I soon found that my taste for rugby drinking and all that goes with it was not going to last. It was no great loss; I played first team hockey and found a new side of me: I wasn't so stupid after all.

My grades at university were good – quite remarkable in light of my previous academic performances. My subject turned out to be the theory behind sport (not running around and being fit as I had anticipated): physiology, biomechanics, psychology. I was fascinated by these topics. I was a good student and I took pride in my grades. So did Dad.

This was where it started to get strange. My father had always wanted to get a university education. After fumbling his way to his teaching certificate, rather like my own route to Higher Education, he had been denied his Master's Degree because of his tuberculosis. Instead, I guess his children would achieve for him. Well, his daughter anyway. But even that had changed. My sister had always sailed through exams: an incessant worrier but intelligent and a natural linguist. But she ran into stormy weather during her teaching degree. She fell in love, several times, and eventually left her course. My sister was happy but my father was deeply upset. But then here was I, the thick, fat one: new and improved, performing, getting good grades. And my father started to wear me like a badge.

I didn't like it one bit. This man was God to me, and every time we went out he would be singing my praises, telling everyone how I was the star now; it was my intelligence against his ignorance. But I didn't want to be like that. Sure, to everyone else, but not him; I didn't want to be better than him.

At the same time, I started to notice things, things that had always been there but must have been hidden behind my adoration. At first it was stupid things like digital watches and videos: phoning me at College to ask for instructions on how to programme the video; waiting until I was at home for vacations so that I could change the digital read out on his watch. These were things he was quite capable of, he just didn't like change.

This resistance to the future, something that I was keenly awaiting, grew. I noticed how when I spoke of serious issues – politics, justice, sexuality – that his views were those of an old man. I had used to hang on every word he said. But now, I saw my father, but I saw him as a racist, a sexist, and a homophobe. He was clearly no longer the man I dreamed of becoming.

As I went on through my undergraduate and Master's degrees the wall where he hung mine and my sister's certificates (she returned to university to qualify as a teacher) became more of a shrine than a part of their lounge. I wouldn't be able to look at that side of the wall, it made me sick inside.

But nowhere more did I, and my sister, notice change than in his relationship with our mother. With his teaching career over, and a house empty of children to guide, to instruct, there was only one person left to dominate: my mother.

My father is a very loving husband. But, and this is a big but, on those occasions that his fuse is lit, his need to be in control, and to be feared and obeyed, illuminate his insecurities and the man becomes nothing but a spoilt boy. For my entire life I had ignored this. I had told myself that good comes with bad. Such a great man must be allowed his vices. I didn't want to accept it; I didn't want to see his weaknesses; and I certainly didn't want to point them out to him. I wanted us always to be the father and son I had dreamed of. We had built a bridge between us and become one and the same. Then one day the bridge collapsed.

The day after, the day after Boxing day. Lying in my bed, listening to his torrent of abuse, I grip the sheets on either side of me and force my face deeper into the pillow. I'm twenty four years old but don't feel a day over nine. Perhaps, if I can just push my face further into the softness, it'll all go away. No use, he's still screaming foul things from the bottom of the stairs, while my mum stands on the landing outside my bedroom door. He covers all the usual stuff: Why do you do this to me? Why don't you just fuck off back to your mum's. I don't work my bollocks off just so you can put me back in debt. You're always doing what I distinctly tell you not to.

Dad had always had a temper. He was never particularly violent, and never with mum. But when he was angry there was a fury you could see in his eye's, and smell on his breath as his bellows would give birth to his rage. But this time was different. This time something came out of his mouth that sealed the lid on the coffin that contained the last remains of the idol he had once been. As he stormed up the stairs and into their bedroom for what seemed like the one hundredth time I heard the words: "Lesley, I want a divorce." And then broken, as if spelling out the sentence, "I – don't – like – you – anymore. Do you understand? You can have the house, I'll get myself a nice little place. I can finally get away from you."

Until this point my mother had been doing rather well. Over the years she's grown used to his anger exploding in her face, and would soak up the abuse like a sponge without getting too upset. As a child I remember she would be sitting, too upset to be able to stand, with her head in her hands crying uncontrollably, while he stood above her, relentless in his sharp, stabbing words. But after years of this I guess you get used to it. This cold December morning, however, was different. Of all the arguments I had been audience to over the years I had never once thought he was truly unhappy. I always knew he would calm down and we would all carefully shuffle through the silent motions of his apology.

By now I'm fully awake. My heart is pounding: the instinctive fear of my father's fury. I get up and quietly walk out onto the landing, unsure of what exactly I'm going to do. Only once had I ever played any part in one of these interactions. Mum had prepared fish for dinner but, knowing I dislike any food that requires delicacy in the process of getting it from my plate to my stomach, had made me lasagne. He was already in a mood and was shouting. He felt that this special treatment was too much; that she was stupid to give herself extra work just so I could eat with a lone fork. The argument was already about to take place, all that was required was the trigger. Then, as if on cue, he got a fish bone in his mouth. He threw his plate on the floor beside me. The precise words that accompanied this action elude me but, not surprisingly, my mother burst into tears and ran up stairs. I sat there for about a minute, quietly furious and ashamedly frightened, then got up and said something like, "I'm not gonna eat my dinner with the likes of you." And with that I took my plate upstairs to see mum. That put him in his place! I was twenty.

He's at the bottom the stairs, still ranting. My mother is sat on the edge of their bed. Her eye's stare straight at me, tears rolling down her cheeks, her lower lip twisted downwards at each end in that way that only happens when we cry uncontrollably, as though the corners of her mouth were trying to wrench themselves from her face while she held onto them for dear life. I'm not sure if she's seen me or whether she's simply staring towards the sounds of my father's voice.

"Do you understand me Lesley? I've had enough." My mother lifts herself from the bed and walks towards me on the landing.

"Jerry stop being so silly you're scaring me..."

"Ssh mum. Go back," I whisper. I hold out my right arm, my hand open, palm towards her to prevent her getting on to the landing. I just can't listen to this anymore. I don't know how many times since I was a child I've had to be an audience to this one-way monologue of insults. I can feel the anger surging round my body. I'm shaking. I now know what I'm about to do and part of me can't believe it. My open hand forms itself into a tightly clenched fist and I take one last deep breath. The moment his face appears above that banister I'm gonna kick the fucking shit out this man; this man who had been, for so many years, everything that was good. And the most frightening thing of all was I wanted to. I wanted to drag the little shit out of the house by the scruff of the neck. He didn't belong here anymore. He didn't deserve her anymore.

He's stood half way up the stairs, still shouting the same vile words he has been all morning. Another two steps and he'll see me, and then they'll be no turning back. Come on you bastard. Come on. He stops again, just below me, probably realising that he's simply repeating himself and really hasn't anything left to say, turns and heads down the stairs, out of the house, and drives away. I'm left, still clenching my fist, relieved and frustrated – somewhere inside of me someone would have enjoyed hurting him. I reassure my mother, shower, pack my stuff, and her an overnight bag, and we're gone.

Until he reads this – if he ever gets to read it – my father won't know how close we came to ending everything.

After bundling my mother and a few things into my van, in an attempt to tell him of my feelings, I left a book by Blake Morrison, *And When Did You Last See Your Father?*, where he would find it. It tells the story of a son watching his father die of cancer. A prominent theme for me is the regret Morrison feels once his father has gone, over all those things he had wanted to say and to question but could never find the courage to. My father read the book and told me he hoped that when he dies I don't feel the same. After a few days my mother went home. We have yet to talk honestly of what happened that Christmas.

The last few years have been a very strange time for me: an unmaking. Sometimes I feel as though he has betrayed me; by not being the superhero he was supposed to have been. Sometimes I just look at him an see an everyday fallible man. At the moment we're just two people, father and son, joined by blood. In my case, a mixed up mess of love and hate. We've gone full circle; once again we're different people.

It was a friend who, after reading parts of this story, pointed out the nature of the metaphor in my original title – *The Body Bridge*. Bridges are unmoving, solid structures. They join two places but they don't bring them any closer together. For those years that both of our sporting bodies could stand up to the strain we shared a truly successful hegemonic, father-son relationship. But as I grew up and he grew older the common ground we had occupied became derelict. The bridge we had built between us became old and decayed. That morning after Christmas it collapsed, dragging most of our relationship back into the chasm we had dragged it from all those years ago.

An Attempt at Closure

This story has stumbled along in its conception and production for years. I never really believed that these words would ever rest on anyone's bookcase. From the beginning I have experienced a sense of guilt because of their existence. There seems an inherent feeling within me that writing of one's father in such a fashion is strictly taboo. Uncovering his weaknesses, while he still lives and breathes, makes me feel as though I have taken the final step of paternal disrespect; that I've broken the male bond completely and 'grassed him up'. Perhaps this is why I have yet to encounter such writings about fathers still alive. Perhaps it is only through death that this bond is broken for us and we are finally allowed to give voice to our grievances in an attempt to close that chapter of our lives. Perhaps it is not until their physical presence is absent that we can conclude the story of our boyhood.

Few stories are ever really finished; instead their content and conclusions are continually revised throughout time. So why then have I written it? At first it was a simple exercise in writing. My brief: to write a story about my body. But the exercise led to reflection on how my relationship with dad had begun to change. And so the story grew, and grew, following my perceptions of my father as he swung to and fro between hero to villain and back again. Its twists and turns bear witness to my struggle to make sense of who I am, who he is, and exactly what he means to me. I've written this story because I'm scared; I'm scared of what has happened; of what I have become, of what he has become; and of what I'm to do about it. I'm scared that if I don't write this story now, then I'll be writing it in ten or twenty years time but it will be too late to share my concerns with him. Perhaps I have found an ending but I'm simply struggling to find a way of telling him. Perhaps I just want to tell him there used to be a time when he was everything to me. That I've seen him fall, witnessed his imperfections, but that I no longer mind. That I've travelled with him for much of this journey, that I know our destinations are different and we will eventually part. That, yes, I am scared about that and of what life will be like without him but that his company is welcome to the very end.

Jim Denison

BOXED IN

For my family, Michael David Madonick, and as always Pirkko

I'll never forget my twenty-first birthday: August 10th, 1984. Not because I got a car or some other big present. It wasn't a happy day... Not a happy day at all.

I was home from college for the summer and I had planned a modest celebration with my high school friends at Calhouns. Calhouns was an Irish pub in Manhattan we patronised on special occasions like birthdays and graduations, and at the beginning of summer vacation. It was a famous spot because IRA operatives supposedly hung out there. But the Olympics from Los Angeles were on television, and two guys I knew, Adeji and Seamus, were entered in the 1500 meter run. So instead I stayed at home with my parents to watch.

My parents didn't know much about running. Skiing and sailing were their sports. They knew running a sub four-minute mile was good (Roger Bannister was the only runner they could name) but they thought that was commonplace these days. Like the way bunches of people climb Everest every year. They also respected anyone who ran a marathon. They considered, Mr Saunders, our neighbour, who ran the New York City Marathon in just under four hours, a good runner. They didn't distinguish between runners and joggers, but I did. They asked me when I was going to run a marathon.

"Not any time soon," I said quickly.

The three of us were sitting around a green wrought iron picnic table in our backyard, eating hamburgers, potato salad, and corn-on-the-cob – my request for my birthday dinner – before moving inside to watch the Games coverage. The early evening air was still; the large oak trees bordering our property wrapped us in shade. A Good Humor truck drove past ringing its bells. In hot pursuit was a young boy shouting wildly, "Stop, Stop, Stop" as if someone was jabbing needles into him.

"You could run a marathon," my father said, lowering his corn to his plate. "On Sundays you run for hours."

"Of course I could run one," I said. "That's not the point. I'm training for the mile and that's different."

Instead of asking what the difference was, my father raised his corn slowly to his mouth as if it weighed something substantial. Drops of butter fell to his plate. I imagined what he was thinking. *Nothing's that complicated. You always make things more difficult than they really are.*

My father used words sparingly. For example, it was because of what he did – fixing her Sanka and washing the dinner dishes; massaging her feet while she read the evening newspaper; and quickly answering the phone Saturday mornings so that she could sleep-in – not what he said, that I knew he loved my mother.

As he brought his corn closer to his mouth – his eyes closed and teeth beared – the ivory candle in the centre of the table shined on it, and it glistened in his hands like a bar of gold. After a few bites he paused, then he stared into my face. His sallow cheeks a soulful backdrop.

"Why do you need to run so much, just to race a mile?" he asked.

I wasn't sure. And I didn't want to say, "Because that's what everyone does." So I said, "It's complicated. It would take a long time to explain." I'm sure he wanted to say, *Son, I'm your father. Can't you talk to me?* But all he did was bite into his corn.

I first met Adeji and Seamus in 1983, in New Orleans, at the National Collegiate Track and Field Championships. We consoled each other in a dingy jazz club off Bourbon Street after we failed to advance to the 1500 meter final. They were different guys, from different lands – Adeji, Nigeria, Seamus, Ireland. But I liked them both. While Adeji said he ran for sheer pleasure and enjoyment, Seamus said he ran to save his life. His father died at forty-two from a massive heart attack. So Seamus was doing his best to stay slim and strong.

When Adeji told me that his father advised him, To become a great sportsman, son, you must love your sport, I remember wishing that my father had given me advice like that. But my Dad spent his childhood reading novels and assembling model planes. His parents dissuaded him from taking up sports. Matters of the mind were more important, they believed. It was my mother who taught him how to ski and sail. She even had an uncle who played semi-pro ball. "It's all from my side," she boasted to me once, "that you got your athletic talent."

I always thought that I learned to ski when I was three years old. When I asked my mother, though, she said I was five. That's still young, I thought. When I told her I couldn't remember much from those early days she began to tell me stories. First she told me how the whole family used to pile into our Country Squire station wagon Friday nights and drive to Vermont for the weekend. She said we'd squeeze into one hotel room and eat leftover spaghetti out of an electric frying pan. Then she told me about the time we rented a fancy condominium on Mount Vesper, when I was seven, and I remembered it. She also told me how I used to throw-up during the drive to Vermont, and I remembered that. Then she described the old brick house between Mount Blackstone and Bear Peak that overlooked a cemetery that we shared with the Fitzgeralds when I was nine, and I remembered that, too.

"You remember more than you think," she said.

She was right. For instance, I remembered that I learned to ski by copying my brother, Mark, who is eight years my senior, the closest in age to me in our family. I used to tuck behind him and watch his body move from side to side to the sound of rushing air. A guide, free, floating, dancing, but also secure. The way the branches on the oak tree in our front yard swayed on a stormy day. The tree I loved to climb when I was a little boy. When my father would shut off the lawn mower to watch me, and Mark and my other older brother Chris would stop cutting the hedge and encourage me to climb higher, and my mother and my older sister Carol would gaze up from weeding the vegetable garden and say, "Be careful, Jimmy, don't climb so high. It's dangerous."

When I skied with Mark I felt looks from the people in the chairs above us. I even imagined their words. *Wow, look at those two*, or, *There are a couple of good skiers.* Just the way I imagined voices when I was out running. Television announcers' voices, calling me in the last 100 meters of the Olympic 1500 meter final. *And the gold medal goes to, Denison!*

On the chair lift Mark would remove his Ray Ban sunglasses to air out his eyes. Then we'd search for other expert skiers and eat hard boiled eggs and Snickers bars to save time stopping for lunch. Once I asked Mark if I could try on his sunglasses. The metal rims were cold against my head. The glasses felt loose and cumbersome. Too big, like a poor disguise. I didn't ask Mark how I looked. I knew from his soft smile and quiet chuckle that to him I looked silly. The way our grey poodle, Rosa, looked when we put a baseball cap on her head, or stuck her front paws inside my Dad's leather wing tip business shoes.

That was how it felt sometimes to be the youngest child. Like a pet, like a plaything. My friends in high school called me an accident because there was such a big gap between my brothers and sister and me. "Typical Irish Catholic mistake," they teased. They were probably right. But I didn't care. It wasn't important anymore. Besides, there were advantages being the youngest, like visiting my brothers at college.

I visited Chris once when I was ten. He was a sophomore at Harvard. He lived in Hancock House. The same house as my Dad. I rode the Amtrack up to Boston all by myself. We went to see the Harvard-Yale football game. It snowed the entire game, and afterwards we went sledding on trays we'd stolen from the cafeteria. It was bitter cold that afternoon, but all I would wear, I remember, was my maroon "H" hooded sweatshirt. The one with Harvard's motto, *Ver-i-tas*, on it. The one Chris gave me for my ninth birthday.

Like Adeji, I also loved how it felt to run fast, to push myself, to be out on my own. But it felt better to be good at something, to beat other people. And after Eddie DeMarco struck me out in the sixth grade with three straight curve balls it wasn't until my freshman year of high school when I ran a mile in gym class and beat everyone that I found something else to be good at. The gym teacher, Mr McMahon, came up to me after class. He said I should go out for the track team. He said I showed promise. When I got home I told my Mom.

"Mom," I shouted, running upstairs to her bedroom, "I'm on the track team."

"That's terrific, dear," she said, laying down her book, and clearing a space on her bed. "Sit here and tell me all about it."

I told her how I beat all the other kids. That I sprinted past them in the last fifty yards. She looked proud. Then I boasted, "I'm going to run in the Olympics one day."

She gasped. "That would be fabulous, dear. I've always wanted to see an Olympic Games opening ceremony. I understand that the pageantry of the parade of athletes marching into the stadium behind their flags and the lighting of the torch is a spectacle that can only be appreciated in person."

As my parents and I listened to the television commentator read the names of the runners for the first heat of the men's 1500 meters, I picked-up the newsletter from my college coach, Mr Garret. Every summer about this time he sent a newsletter to the whole team. Mine usually arrived on my birthday. He never wished me happy birthday, though. Then again, I didn't know when his birthday was. The newsletter contained tips on nutrition and training, nothing I didn't already know, and was full of corny quotes meant to motivate us. "Winning heals all wounds." "Sweat plus sacrifice equals success." That was how Mr Garret spoke. If you went into his office with a problem he'd start reciting a bunch of inspirational sayings. "Adversity makes a man wise, not rich." "He that falls today may rise tomorrow." "Crosses are ladders that lead to heaven." His desk top calender had a different proverb for every day. Each morning he turned the page and read what it said. He wasn't a religious man, but he believed in those bits of wisdom. He said they helped him understand some of the mysteries of life.

I'm not sure what I believe in any more. Up until that Olympic summer of '84 I certainly believed in myself and all the possibilities the future offered. I was turning twenty-one, heading into my senior year of college, ready to make my mark. What could possibly get in the way?

I should have listened when the pain started. But it was hardly anything at all at first. Just an occasional ache, nothing I couldn't tolerate. I kept training on it every day, most days twice. Like I said, it was my senior year and I had big plans. When it started to get bad I swore to myself every night before going to sleep that if it still hurt in the morning

I'd take the day off. Rest it. Give it a chance to heal. But I never did.

Lying in bed the morning of my twenty-first birthday I felt especially hopeful. Today's the day it'll all be over. Today's the day I'll be well again. Overnight I had dreamt that my guardian angel drew my injury away the way a child sucks his soda dry with a straw. So after I swung my feet out of bed and planted them on the floor, I bit my lower lip, closed my eyes, and crossed myself in thanks before standing. But when my first step resulted in its normal stabbing pain I fell back onto my bed and began kicking my legs in the air and pounding my arms on the mattress as if I was trying to smash my way out of a box. Rolling to my right, I grabbed my foot and yanked it towards my face. The Achilles tendon was swollen and hot to touch. Then, staring into it as if I possessed X-ray vision, I began shouting wildly, asking someone, anyone, "What's inside there? What's causing this?" Then growing angrier, and sharpening my stare I screamed, "Go away! Go away! Go away!"

Panting from hurrying upstairs, my mother found me tangled in a heap of sheets with tears streaming down my face. She rushed towards me and began peeling off sheets. Then she enveloped me in her arms and said, "My poor birthday boy. Everything will be all right." For a moment I believed her. Not because I knew she was speaking from experience – my mother had never injured her Achilles tendon – but because in desperate times a person has to believe in someone.

When the television commentator finished saying names I folded the newsletter in half then in half again and put it down and looked at the screen. Adeji was in this heat. I doubted that he or Seamus would advance to the next round, but I wanted to see how they did. To speculate how I might have done.

Adeji moved into good position early, but the pace was slow.

"Take the lead, Adeji," I screamed at the television. "Push it now."

This wasn't his type of race. His finishing kick was poor. He ran best when the pace was fast from the start. With one lap to go I could see that he was in trouble. An Englishman and an Italian were in front of him, and an Australian was on his right.

"Get out of there," I yelled.

My father asked if it was me what I'd do.

"I'd stay out of lane one in such a slow race," I said. "It's too easy to get into trouble there. I'd run the extra distance in lane two so I'd have room to respond when the break occurred."

He nodded. I guess he accepted that as a reasonable reply. Sure enough, when the guys up front started to sprint Adeji had nowhere to go. He was boxed in. And as the leader, a Kenyan, I wasn't sure which one, increased his lead, Adeji slowly drifted out of the picture.

Suddenly I became angry. How could anyone make such a stupid mistake? Couldn't he see what was happening around him? Why didn't he use better judgement? Why didn't he react, or change his tactics? But it was my birthday, my twenty-first birthday, my first day as a fully-fledged, responsible adult, and I wanted to celebrate. So I put on a party hat. A gold crown that said KING across the front. My parents put on hats, too. Now we were having fun.

Between heats of the 1500 meters my mother carried in a cake. Yellow cake with chocolate frosting. Her smile lit up the room as she approached me. Behind her my father held an armload of boxes wrapped in shiny, coloured paper. He placed them beside my feet. As my mother lowered the cake in front of me the top of her head brushed my chin. Her blond hair fell across her cheeks. I had to push it away from the twenty-one candles. It almost caught fire. Then, as she stepped away from me, the cake in place, the candles shining up on her, and her hair falling back to reveal her face, I looked at her and wondered what she must have looked like when she was twenty-one. Next, she started singing. My father joined in. But I didn't hear a word. As soon as they finished I leaned forward to blow out my candles. I froze, though, when I felt a sharp twinge in my right foot. After it passed I squeezed my eyes tight, wished hard, and then blew.

I didn't understand why my Achilles wasn't getting better. Our family doctor told me to ice it after every run, massage it at night, and stretch it all the time. But still it was too sore to touch. Each day I felt it worsening. Each morning I broke the promise I'd made to myself the night before. Take some time off. Rest it. Give it a chance to heal. I felt like I was on top of a big spinning ball. Moving my feet faster and faster, like a logroller, so that I wouldn't slip down any further, so that I wouldn't get squashed by the ball. Nothing frightened me more than that ball rolling over me. It was my senior year. Watching from the sidelines would be impossible to take. But that night, the night of my twenty-first birthday, August 10th, 1984, while I was at home with my parents watching the Olympic Games on television a queer feeling in my gut told me it was too late, that I was in serious trouble. And somehow I knew it to be true. So like a man who senses his lover drifting away, who realises that he's about to get dumped, I began to prepare for the worst.

After only a few bites of birthday cake, I put my plate down. I asked my parents if I could switch channels. I figured I could read in the newspaper how Seamus did. I turned to a documentary about creatures who live on the edge of the sea. Then I started to pray. I sat still in my chair moving my lips in silent repetitive prayer. I didn't know if the All Mighty Father cared if people ran fast, but I figured He wanted us to be well, to win, to be happy. That was why I prayed. In the background I heard my mother ask me when I was going to open my presents. I also heard the television commentator describing the different varieties of sea urchins. She said that there were 850 living species, and that generally they live deep within the moss, and in holes and depressions in the coral rock, their globular bodies anchored securely to the underlying rock by adhesive discs. Many are dark purple or green, or intense shades of red and orange. I remember her specifically mentioning two varieties of sea urchins, the long-spined sea urchin, and the slate-pencil urchin. Contrary to what people think, she added, most sea urchins aren't poisonous. However, a few fishermen and swimmers do die each year from stings.

My mother prayed for me my whole senior year. Whenever I phoned home she asked me how my Achilles was.

"Are you running yet, dear?"

"No, Mom," I'd tell her. "My Achilles still hurts."

"Well, I'm praying for you. Your father and I are saying a rosary novena every night for you."

I didn't tell her that I'd stopped praying, that I'd given-up believing that I'd ever be well again. Instead, I thanked her and said, "I'm sure I'll be running again soon, Mom."

Peter Swan

THREE AGES OF CHANGING

Introduction

The notion of epiphany is the best way for me to encapsulate the way in which this paper has been written in that, many of my significant life experiences are embedded in sport, and the culture that surrounds it. (Swan 1998) I transferred (like a professional sports player does) from a normal secondary schooling to a career in human movement (see physical education) which was, and still is, shrouded in masculinising practices that 'hegemony' was invented to describe. I absorbed these practices into myself as ink to blotting paper. Thirty years later and not a lot has changed in Australia (me thinks), except, thankfully, me! The use of nostalgic humour can mask many of the alienating aspects of sports participation, but also, it is an essential part of the lens through which I interpret my experiences.

The physical space set aside for changing into sports attire and vice versa is a site for the practice of body techniques (Crossley 1995) as embodied forms of action, often requiring specific rituals, and is often passed beyond (Van Den Berg 1964) in silence, meaning that the body is forgotten, or left behind as the performance becomes pre-eminent. As a result of continual knee surgery, and finally, a tibial osteotomy, combined with the knowledge that I could never run again, that when left in the change-room with the reality of my body and its vulnerability, I commenced to write about these wondrous places. However readers need be wary of my uncertain eye, "as it is only via the abstract imaginary of the human sciences that catalogues and museums action, constituted through academic writing that techniques (read change-rooms) assume a generalised, atomised and decontextualised form." (Van Manen 1997). Lived experience is simply different to the tales written about such experience.

The following narrative is about two change-room experiences and my cataloguing of those experiences. Whilst this story is interesting, the beyond storyness, that is, the reflection upon the story as written and my musings over the story strike me as equally important. The background to these stories is real, based upon hundreds of hours of participant observation and a somewhat untrustworthy 'grounded theory'.

The first change-room story sat in the repository part of my mind that is jumbled with ideas, misgivings and apprehension. Amidst the discussions I had about this story I began to question how I came to see things this way. How was the story related to my own life history? I played ethnography. What a fine game. one where you partially make the rules, To enable the reader into my thinking about the story entitled "Three Ages of Changing", I have included a series of interrupted readings that are reflective and questioning of the very essence of the story and how I came to see things in that light.

The First Story

I didn't know that there was one age of changing, let alone three, until I joined the local YMCA (Young Men's Christian Association), I moved quickly between the reception area where the aerobics instructors chatted between classes. I always admired the way they took my membership card from me without recognising, or looking at me at all. Not even a pause in their conversation. I looked them up and down, scored them out of ten, lapsing, I leered over them; and they didn't even know that either! In most situations where I meet people I am able to attract their attention, I feel very neglected here and immediately think it is both a matter of age and bodies. The change-room was humid and tiled all over, the floors and walls and it had athletes' photos mounted on the wall. The imagery of Nike, Reebok and Speedo created a powerful allure. The photos were of elite sportswomen or luscious models (are they the same?) with a dominant focus upon (...) you know where! I guessed that the female change-room was full of similar male images. I had a love-hate -relationship with this place. I loved the showers, but I hated the ever constant smell of the urinal. Why don't men and boys flush? Why doesn't the YMCA put fresh dunny blocks there so it isn't quite so evil? I always got changed and found that I then needed a pee. With bare feet and a sense of resignation I move toward the pissoire. Standing in and around someone else's smelly pee has to be a good character builder. Signage of *Please make sure you shower, toilet and blow your nose before swimming*, created a little guilt in me, but two out of three isn't too bad.

Interrupted Reading

As a person with bodily resources that enabled participation in sport at a high level of intensity the change-room was a ritual space where the forthcoming competition was akin to 'battle,' where there was a spatial separation from everyday life. The same feelings of sick stomach, dry mouth and muscular weakness still persist and invade my body as I prepare for a one kilometre swim at a leisure centre! Such conditioning both perplexes and amuses me.

As I walked back to my self appointed changing spot I saw the old man who had been clogging up the swimming lane I had been using. He wasn't that slow, he was doing it (clogging) just because lane rules were unimportant to him. You might be doing eight laps to his two but if you finished at the same time he would push off from the end with impunity, naive bliss and a sense of unstoppability. Just like the fucking Titanic! After we exchanged the glance and nod of generations, which were close enough to do such things, I went to my patch. I looked across to see him sitting on the slatted bench. He was naked except for a thermos (vacuum flask) cap he was drinking from. His body contrasted with the straight edges of the bench; he was round, all round. He leaned forward to rest his forearms along his thighs and he sipped his thermos elixir with such a totally transfixing suck that I was clearly staring. The thermos was an instrument of my parent's generation; any drive over thirty minutes warranted a thermos to be packed. McDonalds and Kentucky Fried have taken over for many, but the site of an elderly couple having a cup of tea from the car boot, by the highway, brings an engulfing wave of melancholia to me.

His hair had been combed with such neatness over so many years that you could now see a wide, bald seam. His gravity assisted, sagging body showed a small tattoo on his arm and a bypass scar that went right down the front of his chest. My eyes kept shifting to all these things to keep his scrotum out of my gaze and mind, for it hung over the front of the bench; it seemed somehow obscene to my eye because he wasn't actively getting changed, he was simply resting, sitting and drinking in a place where you didn't do any of that. He occasionally towelled at a foot; dabbed Johnson's Baby Powder on his feet in such a way that it resembled what I thought a meat inspector would be like in an abattoir. I was ready to go to the pool and swim my life away in that sea of calm, but he somehow transfixed me. Surely this is not what I would be doing over the next twenty years? Maybe he's a 'Mervyn', (rhythming slang) for perving (sexual deviate) at the kids. I swam with a vigour that was borne of Merv's absence from my lane, but I couldn't stop thinking about that change-room. Rushed as I always felt, I only had time to swim a bit over thirty minutes and to my great surprise when I returned to the change room he was just leaving. His green corduroys hung somewhat shapelessly from his waist, he acknowledged my return with a simple statement, "good swim", I nodded and "mmmmed", then smiled. I kept thinking about the people who would have passed through the change-room in that thirty minutes, what did they think of him, his 'ball bag' and that thermos?

Try as I did to remove the image when I got home, Uncle Merv, as I called him, was stuck in my mind like a song. However, I came to better understand his ritual, as the YMCA became a large part of my life over the next six months. I too lingered and took refuge there, I swam a little more, I had a cup of coffee – in the Cafe, not in the change-room – and talked to anyone I could.

Many times I tried to avoid the times when school groups were there, but this was not always possible. They didn't smell bad, and they didn't do much wrong, but there is something about a group of twenty thirteen and fourteen year old boys' that makes you question the future of humanity. They were excited, full of bravado, and so loud. They delved into their bags and all manner of things fell forward. The floor ended up littered with lunch bags and little scraps of paper that came from nowhere. Merv wasn't here to day but I thought of him as I wondered how the school group and he would encounter each other with respect to Merv's free-swinging scrotum. I became annoyed when I saw that the school group was to take up five lanes and 'us' lap swimmers only had two, and with me the only devotee of lane etiquette I knew I was in for a lousy swim.

Interrupted Reading

Recovering from surgery, using callipers (even entry ladders into the pool) I felt myself to be in a new world where my body damage had actually changed me. Self and body were juxtaposed and incoherent. I felt the invisible gaze of all strangers and they left me feeling insecure. My bodily process of 'becoming', unravelled in the change -room as my body techniques created empathy and pity on the part of others, or so I felt. To move beyond myself and interpret the actions of others in relation to my damage and repair situation had become part of my personae.

Upon Returning to the Change Room

The schoolboys were furtive, nervous, anxiously looking over their shoulders as they began a ritual that I was to witness upon many occasions. I called it 'the cocoon'. With great precision they all placed their towels around their waist and commenced what can only be called the difficult procedure of removing their wet togs from under the towel and then getting their undies over that sticky flesh. Was it their 'little' appendages and emerging pubescence, or genetic predisposition that enforced this ritual. Some took to the toilets; locking the doors and ensuring no eyes were upon them. Usually the first few to finish began to torture others by tugging threateningly at their towels. It looked so funny to see boys being modest about anything. Clearly it was a passing phase related to 'altering fixtures'. Early maturers and late, it didn't seem to matter, they all did it. The most amusing aspect of this was the looks that all cocooners took over their shoulder, they were '*am I being followed*? -type looks' straight out of detective movies. It was hard to know where not to look as change room etiquette demands. *No eye*

41

contact — Definitely no eye to appendage contact and — No excessive drying of particular body parts.

Consequently, many males leave change-rooms wet, half-dressed and with a sense of surprised relief that is borne of fear. For the life of me I could not remember whether I had been a cocooner. Is this cultural body technique peculiarly Australian and part of our relations in public?

Perhaps this seems like the story of a voyeur, but I hasten to note, that as a sports participant for over thirty-five years change-rooms are a place I can evaluate with ease. Showers, tiling, (do I need to wear thongs?), smelly, creepy (what is that bloke looking at?), wet under-foot, mirrors etc. Also I was a malingerer, keen to get off the training track and spend luxury time in the change room resting. So forgive my interest in these wondrous places.

With Merv and the Cocooners floating around in my mind I began the strange classification that only an ethnographic admirer could find of interest. The questions that led me to many others were; at which stage do we prefer to sit down to get changed? Did Cocooners become like Merv? And more significantly, why was Merv such a rare being? There were so few older people around this place.

Somewhere between the two phases discussed so far must be added the 'mirror seekers'. This group of changers tended to be about 18 - 30 years of age and in desperate need of a mirror fix. Changing, after a weight workout, for this group was a matter of noticing the position of the mirrors and ensuring proximity to appropriate reflections. This group always combed their hair and used the hair drier whilst naked, and they had a strut related to the difficulty they had getting their thighs together. Towelling for this group was vigorous, looked painful and was done with vigour borne of excessive energy. The towel was held at either end and dragged like a saw across all sections of the body, and the action between the legs looked particularly abrasive. I was often tempted to ask one of them whether drying was part of their exercise schedule, but I didn't. Nudity was neither central nor peripheral but rather a part of body maintenance and development. The calf muscle was of equal modifiable capacity as the nose, butt and don't forget dimples can be added (in the chin). "A wider penis should be no prob-lem, sir. Are you happy with sir's length?" I think I have maligned this third age of changers for no greater reason than their pre-occupation with appearance, bodies and their arrogance.

Interrupted Reading

Just as Shilling (1993) points to the value we place upon the exterior surfaces of bodies (youth, looks, sexuality etc) so I added the notion of the body on display (Goffman 1972) to highlight the need that 'mirror seekers' have for the attention of others to enable them to act in public and I was an unwitting part of their audience.

Cocoons, Mirrors, and Mervyns are very inadequate descriptions of change room behaviours. That young males can feel so susceptible to the 'gaze' of others says much about societal expectations. The issue of change room design has often been mentioned as a factor affecting female participation in school based sport and physical education. Male change rooms in schools are barn like structures with no nooks and crannies, and may be an equally important factor affecting male participation, although this would be strongly denied.

My last image of changing probably reflects a change in me. I was towelling off after a dip; quick to do that, so those clothes could be draped upon my middle-aged frame. As I was doing so the deserted change room was entered by a 7–8 year old who was absolutely distraught, sobbing, groaning and wailing. I watched, started to move toward him to see if I could help. I realised from outside my body that this would not be a clever thing to do in this era of child abuse. I have to admit that I panicked and threw my clothes on whilst I was wet. No one entered the rooms and I eventually moved over to this shivering, distraught bundle: "Are you alright, son?" I inquired. He looked up at me and replied: "No, I'm having a nervous breakdown, I just can't cope. I'll never pass level five swimming." What could I say, he had diagnosed himself brilliantly given the symptoms, no simple hurt feelings or skinned knees for this generation.

Cocoons Take on a Different Meaning

Upon my return to work I became involved with an action research project. The following 'story' about changing arose as a consequence of that study in a Catholic Secondary school on aspects of health promotion. The study appeared to be totally unrelated both in method and involvement to the ethnographic fiction about changing that I was narrating, except that the action research group (year 7-12 students) became interested in having changing cubicles in the boys change-room. Their interest in the cubicles arose in an effort to encourage higher levels of participation in school-based sport and physical education. It was school policy that the boys had to change for sport and physical education as well as shower afterwards. The current lack of privacy was seen as a factor that affected participation. We agreed that we would see how significant this issue was to boys who didn't participate very much. Purposeful sampling led us to six boys, including Bryan. These are the interview words of Bryan – *Changing (for) Bryan* – in loose verse format. They arose from the question I asked: "Bryan could tell me a little about your experiences in sport and physical education at school?"

Well, because of how I'm perceived at school
It's most uncomfortable, you know, ridicule and teasing and stuff.

From year eight on, they'd call it 'jokes'.
"Why don't you come and get me poojammer,"
"Take a look at this one needle-dick."
"Oh you faggot, ah, perving are you."

They reckon I'm skinny, I act and can dance,
The clothes I wore are the same as theirs
You know, I hate ridicule and teasing and stuff.

I always worried about the change-room,
and, and, and (...)
what's going to happen in the showers?
Yuk, I don't want to do sport or PE.
Like, they make advances in
A dirty kind of ridicule way.

A hundred times I left my gear at home
Lots of notes from mum or from me!
I was sick in my stomach over sport and PE
I got a lot of detentions, some poor reports too.
It's the shower part that was really so bad,
"He's gonna fuck you, it's backs to the wall"

They'd spit and pee on me
I'm really weak when it comes to violence and that stuff.

I'd be saved if they teased Sam because of his weight
He'd just laugh at the fat jokes, others too, because of their tool,
How far they'd matured
"No pubes, tree trunk, pin dick and things like that."
It's uncomfortable, ridicule teasing and stuff.

You need to be able to do things that
Don't make you have to shower if you don't want to.
Teachers feel bad so they don't go in
People would grab me and simulate sex..
When I got older I could deal with it then.

In primary school I'd go home crying and hated school lots
At junior high I got blamed for not doing sport
But now it doesn't grab me at all
You know (...) the ridicule, teasing and stuff.

Methodological Sidetrack

When I began to read extended interview text in amongst academic proffering I honestly get lost. There is little sense of the power of narrative, the feeling of lived experience or the drama of ordinary lives. This is particularly the case when interviewer and study participant are intermingled as follows:

> Peter:.blah blah – Researcher: blah blah, blah – Peter: blah, blah blah (...)

Richardson (1991, 126; 1994) discusses the difficulty in reading a great deal of research papers that are not really written with the reader in mind. She argues that, "the culture suppresses and devalues its members subjective experiences. For example, we are expected to write papers in prose, reference others and place our work in a lineage, objectify the topic and focus on the expressed topic rather than on the self as producer." Sparkes (1995) discusses the notion that by choosing to use poetry as a representative format the author is able to see familiar sites in new ways.

I have tried (Swan 1998) to use forms of verse that allow the reader to feel the emotional context of the data and to produce a story. Clearly, poetry may better represent the speaker, whilst at the same time problematising trustworthiness. There is no plot in this poem, as in narrative, yet voice is given to the reader to make sense, to feel and to rupture the tranquillity of assumed relationships. *Changing (for) Bryan* arose from three pages of interview notes. Upon reading it Bryan expressed that he was very happy, that the words were very much his and he then said: "Make sure Endo and Jerker (two physical education teachers) read it won't you." He felt let down.

Bryan's Story, Cocoons and Consequences to Me

I too feel the reality of my body and its vulnerability in the change-room as I sit precariously perched between two worlds. One world where I feel my acutely flawed body, not only damaged by earlier conquests in sport but ravaged by lifestyle. It is with a sense of urgency that I seek the 'other world' where my body is passed over, where my performative competence body enables my body (on display) to be silenced. As I swim I silence my internal detractors and imaginary others in a manner that never ceases to please me as I begin to lose myself in a sea of embalmed calm that is long distance swimming. But this attempt on my part to reconcile self and body, to seek coherence, strikes me as useful to me alone. Oppression of boys like Bryan strikes at us all. Bryan as a metaphor for a marginalised version of masculinity suffers immensely

Boys change-rooms in school settings are like testing laboratories, proving grounds for the dominant model of masculinity. The constitution of masculinity in these change-rooms is not so much bodily performance (Connell 1995) but an opportunity to make/focus embodied emotions into objectifications. A public sorting house in which selfhood is at stake and able to placed into a competitive arena by others. Humour is an organisational principle in the sporting and schooling experiences of young men (Kehily & Nayak 1997) and is regulatory in that masculinity is not so much a positive or conscious construct, rather as a counter to that which is feminine and more particularly effeminate. In this context the attributes of hegemonic masculinity that include aggression, power, competitiveness, strength and individualism are felt by Bryan as domination, ridicule, bullying and power relations. I am sure that there would be many boys who would not actively participate in the ridicule and teasing that boys like Bryan receive. There needs to be counter narratives that support such difference.

References

Connell, R. (1995) *Masculinities*. Allen & Unwin: Sydney.

Crossley, N. (1995) Body techniques, agency and intercorporeality: On Goffman's Relations in Public. *Sociology* (29) 1, 133-150.

Goffman, E. (1972) *Relations in public*. Harmondsworth: Penguin.

Kehily, M. J. & Nayak, A. (1997) Lads and laughter: humour and the production of heterosexual hierarchies. *Gender and Education. Special issue: Masculinities in Education* (9) 1, 69-88.

Richardson, L. (1991) The consequences of poetic representation. In: C. Ellis & M. Flaherty (Eds.) *Investigating subjectivity: Research on lived experience*. London: Sage, 125-137.

Richardson, L. (1994) Writing: A method of inquiry. In: N. Denzin & Y. Lincoln (Eds.) *Handbook of qualitative research*. London: Sage, 516-529.

Shilling, C. (1993) *The body and social theory*. London: Sage.

Sparkes, A. (1995) Writing people; Reflections on the dual crisis of representation and legitimation in qualitative inquiry. *Quest* (47) 2, 158-195.

Swan, P. (1998) Dreaming up, dreaming through and dreaming of people, places and paraphenalia, In: C. Hickey, L. Fitzclarence & R. Matthews (Eds.) *Gender, Sport and Education*. DCEC-Publication. Geelong: Deakin University.

Van Den Berg, J. H. (1964) The significance of human movement. *Philosophy and Phenomenological Research* (13), 159-183.

Van Manen, M. (1997) From Meaning to method. *Qualitative Health Research* (7), 345-369.

David Jackson

BOXING GLOVE

My father couldn't stand a soft, moist palm.
Didn't want to sense his own grip slither
from who he thought he was.

He crammed my uncalloused skin
down into the blooded glove. My bunched,
wriggling fingers curved into pumped-up fist.

He couldn't stretch to his full height
until my skinny wrists were tightly
held in stiff leather.

His own treacherous longings-singing,
dancing, playing the piano like Charlie Kunz –
were hidden behind his hearty shoulder-thump.

A I soldiered on, through round after round,
pummelling my way out from the sneers,
my fighting hands froze into claws.

My fingers aren't mine any more.
I turn away from my father's searching hand.
Too proud to unclench a rock-hard fist.

SHOCKING BODY

Andrew C. Sparkes

THE FRAGILE BODY-SELF

Introduction

"Bodily experiences are often central in memories of our lives, and thus our understanding of who and what we are." (Connell 1995, 53)

"Even though my body seems the most private and hidden part of me, I carry my life history in my body, almost like the way the age rings of a sawn tree trunk reveal a process though time. My personal history of social practices and relationships is physically embodied in the customary ways I hold my body, relate to it, imagine its size and shape, and its daily movements and interactions." (Jackson 1990, 48)

Sometime in 1994 I began to write a story, a narrative of self, from my position then as a 38 year old, white, heterosexual, 'middle class', male, with a 'failed ' body who had memories of an earlier elite, performing, working class body, that housed a 'Fatal Flaw' in the form of a chronic lower back problem. This flaw terminated, very early on, my involvement in top class sport and has remained a companion who has revealed itself in and through me on a regular basis since I was 20 years of age. It has led to numerous bouts of manipulative therapy by osteopaths and chiropractors to keep me mobile and alleviate acute episodes of pain, four series of sclerosing injections into the ligaments around my lumbar vertebrae, two courses of epidural injections, one manipulation under general anaesthetic, and surgery on my lumbar spine in 1988 and 1994 to remove prolapsed discs. Acute episodes of back pain still intrude on my life. I have good days and bad days. Here are some moments from the story I wrote back then.

Thoughts from an Untidy Office

It is May 1994. I have walked down this hospital corridor many times before. The navy blue carpet is familiar as are the polished hand rails on either side. Determined not to use these hand rails for support, I hobble down an imaginary center line. My body is unable to stand up straight, the hips are pulled to one side, and each time I take a step a searing burst of pain unleashes itself in the lumbar region of my back and travels down my right leg. It's hot in the hospital and I'm sweating. I'm also crying and afraid. In 1988 I had surgery on my lumbar spine here for a prolapsed disc and now I have the feeling that the hospital is soon going to swallow me up again. I want it to; I want this pain to be taken away.

Stopping for a rest I turn towards Kitty, my partner, who is 6 months pregnant. "Deja vu", I say to her, "It's happening again". The tears well up in her eyes and we hold each other close in the corridor. I kiss the tears on her cheeks. I kiss her eyes; I want to drown and be saved in the blueness of those eyes. As the roundness of her stomach presses against me, a wave of guilt washes over me. Kitty is pregnant, so tired, caring for Jessica our daughter (3 years old at the time), and now having to worry and cope with the stress of me and my body failure. My uselessness makes me angry with my body. At that moment I HATE it intensely.

That night, as in previous nights since this latest episode with my back started, I lie there focussed on pain. It is impossible to lie on my back. The only position I can get 'comfortable' in is on my side with several pillows tucked between my knees and my thighs. Despite the painkillers, the electric shocks bombard my lumbar area, shoot down both legs, and sometimes intrude into my groin. After an hour, sleep has still not arrived, so I roll myself out of bed as quietly as I can so as not to wake Kitty. Going next door into my 'office' (the only un-decorated room in the house with all my books and my computer), I make myself as comfortable as I can in the orthopaedic chair that the

Social Services supplied me with in 1988 following my first back operation. I sit there, holding some vague notion that if I can do some 'work', that is academic writing or reading, then I'd be making 'good use' of my time. It would be a defiant gesture to my back that it hadn't taken over my life completely; it might also take my mind off the pain. I reflect how, in moments like these, I see the lumbar region of my back and the pain it generates as both part of me and not part of me, as both intimate and alien, as self and other, but one powerful symbol amongst many of the multiple dualisms and contradictions that I inhabit in relation to my body.

Moments from My Medicalised Disease Story

Episode 1

CT Scan of lumbar spine
Date: 18-11-88

Report: Consecutive images between L3 and S1 were recorded. The striking initial feature is a developmental spinal stenosis.

At L3/4 there is evidence of disc degeneration with a broad based annular bulge extending back into the neural canal. This is of significant proportions and extends across to the right and dips below the upper end plate of L4. Facet joints are broadened with minor osteophytosis.

At L4/5 similar features are shown. The disc is narrowed with a broad based bulge extending back into the neural canal. There is probably a partial extrusion of part of the disc, best appreciated on scan 16. Again there are broadened facet joints with thickening of the Ligamenta Flava.

At L5/S1 there is some evidence of degenerative disc disease, however there is a high termination to the sacral sac, and no convincing evidence of nerve root or thecal sac compression is seen. Facet joint osteoarthritis is present.

Summary: The most striking feature is a developmental spinal stenosis with significant acquired stenotic features due to disc disease at L3/4 and L4/5.

Episode 2

Magnetic Resonance Image Scan
Date: 20-5-94

Type of examination: MRI of the lumbar spine.
Clinical history: Micro-discectomy 1988. Recurrence of right leg pain with scoliosis.

Report: The lower three discs are degenerate. At L4/5 there is now a small right sided disc protrusion effacing the anterior epidural fat at the level of the inferior aspect of the disc (please see image with the blue dot). There is no obvious enhancement with Gadolinium to suggest that this is due to scar tissue. No significant disc bulge or protrusion is seen at either of the other two degenerate levels.

Conclusion: Disc protrusion right side L4/5.

Dear Brother.
Telephone Conversation December 1994

Andrew: Can you help me out? I'm trying to get a fix on just what it is that I've got in terms of my back. How would you describe it as an osteopath?

Martin: It all depends who you are talking to, a doctor, an insurance company or somebody else.

Andrew: OK, but what would you say? Am I ill?

Martin: No, not ill. I wouldn't say that.

Andrew: Well, diseased then. It says on the records 'degenerative disc disease'.

Martin: That depends. I could examine lots of men your age and find evidence of that, or the early signs of arthritis. But it's normal for that to happen so I'm not sure if I'd call it diseased.

Andrew: So what have I got?

Martin: I'd say you've got, and suffer from, a chronic inflammatory back condition that goes through acute phases. Like you are at the moment and when you have had the discs prolapse and needed operations.

Andrew: So I'm not ill in your sense.

Martin: No, but you have got a fucked-up back that pisses you off! Anyway, who are you giving all this to?

Andrew: I'm having to give a talk in couple of weeks and I'm trying to use myself as an example of the way that people with chronic problems or conditions, or what have you, try and make sense of what has happened to them. I wish I'd never sent the abstract off because I'm finding it difficult to find the words to write about how I feel. In fact I don't know how I feel, we don't seem to have a language to go with that stuff. At least I don't anyway.

The Fatal Flaw

Saturday morning, December 11th, 1993. Exeter is packed with Christmas shoppers. The crowded streets and shops make me feel claustrophobic. The gym didn't open until 10 am, so I decided to have a coffee. Sitting there I watched the people around me in a detached way. This detachment symbolised a view of myself that had become familiar to me of late. A detachment from a body and a self that were causing me problems, a body and a self that I didn't like too much. Of course, much of this was to do with the usual tiredness and exhaustion that goes with academic work these days and the end-of-term blues. But it was hitting me more than usual. My periods of depression were getting more regular and deepening. Following an extremely stressful period at work where I felt badly treated and let down by my colleagues, I had suffered a severe bout of depression that led to medication and visits to the psychology department at the hospital. Indeed, as part of a move to counteract the overwhelming feeling that I was losing my way and 'cracking up', I had decided to join a gym and begin training again.

I had previously joined this gym when I first came to Exeter in 1988. Then, when I entered I was well muscled from training in other gyms. I was confident enough to work out in an athletics top, and go into the separate room where the loose weights were stored. This area, the loose weights rather than the multi-gym, was where 'serious' trainers went to join together in ritual grunting and grimaces as inanimate iron confronted moving, growing muscle. I enjoyed that feeling – not as a serious hardcore bodybuilder but as someone who could conquer the weights and make them work for me, mould my body, shape myself in a way that I wanted as far as it was possible given the restrictions I was operating under. It was also one of the few activities that I could push myself in and get the 'buzz' of intense exercise. I suppose that the weights were choosing me rather than me choosing them. However, I needed to foster the illusion that I was in control.

Those were confident times, when I knew the atmosphere, the smells, the sounds, the colours of gyms, and felt comfortable in the spaces they occupied in my life. I also felt comfortable about the space my body occupied in my life – not as muscled as it could have been. After all, I could no longer do leg squats or leg curls as this put to much strain on the back. But I was holding things together in a corporeal sense. All this contrasted to my feelings as I entered a gym again after a 5-year break following surgery to my lumbar spine in 1988. As I pushed open the door, a wave of apprehension swept over me. I wanted to walk away. I didn't, and went through the ritual of being shown around by the machines and weights. Moving around the gym I began to feel a bit like when you meet an old friend, or an ex-lover, whom you have parted from on bad terms. You acknowledge each other but little more. Memories of good times gone bad can be too hurtful to resurrect.

A few days after my visit, I had returned to the gym and paid my money for the monthly membership. As part of the membership, you were entitled to regular fitness tests to assess your current physical state and check on your progress. To the uninitiated this test might have seemed impressive – nose clip on, tube in mouth, heart monitor on, computer readings, fat readings, and so on. My background in physiology and research methods told me it was a joke. For example, the 'trainer' measured my thigh circumference while I had my tracksuit bottoms on. It all had an air of absurdity in terms of accuracy and validity. So why did I do the test? Why did I go though with it? I think it was because I wanted some indication that I was still something like I was before, something of what I used to be. I wanted some indication no matter how inaccurate the readings. But to my horror, I remember my embarrassment when the trainer gave me the results from the Astrand/Hodgson scale of cardiovascular fitness, the reading was

POOR. I had never scored POOR on any physical fitness test in my life. But of course it wasn't accurate, was it? Knowing this didn't help, but simply confirmed to me the fears about my physical self in recent years – 38 years old, unfit, out of shape and getting worse.

So I joined the gym and worked out a programme for myself that concentrated on getting my heart rate up using the treadmill, bike and step-machine. Each time I walked into the gym, I felt as though I didn't belong. I didn't want people to see me and chose times of the day when it was not busy. The lean, fit, and muscular bodies that surrounded me, announcing their healthy vitality – their quest for perfection – intimidated me in a way that they could not have done some years ago when I was like them, and better.

That day was to be my third session. As I finished my coffee and got up, I felt a familiar tingle in the middle of my lumbar spine and the muscles began to contract slightly. The fatal flaw had come back into my life again. Perhaps as some perverse attempt to defeat its inexorable progress, I still went to the gym to train. I rationalised my stupidity by not going on the treadmill (a high impact exercise) but doubling up my time on the exercise bike. In the shower afterwards I could feel my back tightening. That night some friends came for a meal, and the wine alleviated the pain for a while. But the next morning reminded me that things were taking their normal course. My back was stiff, walking and bending were painful, and my hips were twisted to one side. My options were a visit to the osteopath or to the specialist to get some relief and get me moving again, until the next time the fatal flaw let me down as I knew it would.

Dear Diary 1994

In April 1994 Kitty, Jessica, and I went for a holiday in Spain. While we were there I began to get a nagging pain in my lumbar region. On returning to England things got progressively worse. The pain became intense, and walking became more and more difficult. Prior to seeing the specialist and having another operation in June, I kept a diary – the first time I have ever done so in my life. Here are a few extracts from the early part of May.

Andrew C. Sparkes

Saturday May 7th, 1994

Kitty drove Jessica and me into town to do some shopping. I am walking so slowly I have to tell them to go on ahead and I will meet them at various points for coffee. I felt intimidated by the speed at which people seemed to be moving in relation to me. I was afraid of being bumped or knocked with a shoulder. I'm experiencing fragility once again and I think back to a time in 1988 just before my first operation. I needed to walk into town to get some money from the building society. It normally would have took 10 minutes. But in my hobbling state it took me 45 minutes. On the way there I had to pass the car and body repair workshop of the local college. Some of the 'lads' were sitting outside in their overalls having a cigarette. As I hobbled by one of them said to his mate "Look at that wanker". I don't think he would have said that if I had been upright and walking normally. If he had, I would have confronted him. Now he felt free to say it. There would be no consequences for him as I could do nothing. I remembered feeling an intense vulnerability that rocked my sense of masculinity to its roots.

An elderly woman is coming out of a shop. She is limping in a similar pattern to me. We cross trajectories like some infirm ballet dancers. We do not acknowledge each other, but I feel embarrassed at our similarities in gait and our differences in age. I feel that people are looking at me, but as I catch their eyes they look away.

Sunday May 8th, 1994

Trying to play with Jessica I felt subdued. Her energetic movements caused me physical pain at times as she pushed or pulled me as we 'tumbled' in the front room. I felt she was getting bored with me, or was she just tired? I felt a sense of detachment from what was going on around me. Mid-afternoon, Jessica wanted to go and play in the park. I couldn't face the pain of the 200 metre walk down the road, so Kitty took her. I felt left out and began wondering what Jessica was making of me. I wondered what use I was to Kitty who was pregnant and now had me as an additional burden and source of stress. What would I be like when the new baby arrived? Would I be the active father I wanted to be in the future?

Monday May 9th, 1994

Walking is slow and very painful. Someone has a knife in my right hip and is slashing it down my leg till it comes out of my toes. I'm very tired due to not being able to sleep at night. I shuffle. This is pronounced given that I don't look injured. Walking to the university shop to get some cigarettes (I'm smoking a lot now), several students see me. They nod, but don't say anything. I feel uncomfortable in their gaze. Perhaps they feel so in mine. Around 11am I need to go to staff house for coffee. People are sitting on the lawn, an area I have named the 'Grass Arena' after an autobiography by John Healy (1988), across from my office and I have to walk by them. I take something to read as I shuffle by so I don't have to make eye contact. People walk by me, they are visibly faster which accentuates my slowness. I feel my own slowness.

Several students walk up to me from behind saying "You look in a bad way". I joke about the dilemmas of aging. They laugh, I laugh, they move on. As they do I resent their youth, their muscularity, their well toned, tanned legs in their baggy shorts. I resent my own body and what it makes me look like in front of them. Their ease of movement offends me by reminding of my distance from a self I used to be in performance terms. I recognise my own alienation from others and my own body. I feel the judgment of an elitist able-bodied culture press upon me, "You do not belong in the Grass Arena – stick to the edges." I also begin to recognise that the oft quoted private/public divide does not operate when you have a limp. The broken, visibly impaired body you carry transcends all contexts. My private pain is also a public pain. Does my being there transgress the norms of this culture? Do I make them feel uncomfortable? Am I a reminder to them of what could happen to them?

Tuesday May 10th, 1994

Moving very slowly towards my office, I meet another member of staff. We dislike each other and do not get on well. Normally we manage to avoid each other whenever possible. Now as she walks by me she smiles and stops to say: "This is the Subject Chair of PE, what an advert – 'Sport is good for you'". I don't think she meant it maliciously, but my disabledness seemed to have created a space for her to move into where a conversation did take place and a joke was cracked as well. But I was the joke.

Other comments were made today as I hobbled about. One from a male colleague was significant. He told me: "You look well and truly fucked." This made me think of a chapter called 'Active sports: The anus and it's goal posts' in the book *Male Impersonators* by Mark Simpson. Its about masculinity, men, and sport. Its about being about those who are the fuckers (the winners) and those who are the fucked the (losers). To be a 'real' male is to be the fucker while to be feminine or gay is to be the fucked. Was I now being defined by others as the fucked? Am I now defining myself as the fucked? What does all this tell me about who I am, who they are, and the person I might be tomorrow?

Wednesday May 11th, 1994

I manage to get an appointment to see the locum of Dr. X. My desire to get a verdict or some indication of what is going wrong makes me drive up the motorway recklessly. In front of the young, suntanned, attractive female locum I became intensely aware that my body was not as I would like it to be under her gaze. I felt awkward physically. But more than this I am aware of my own bodily contours, or lack of them, and the flesh that I do not want on me. This is exemplified when she helps me put on a velcro belt around my waist for the traction machine. As she pulls the belts tight I look down and see some folds of flesh exude above the rim of the belt. I am appalled at my lack of conditioning. At the end she helps me up by my arm. I do not like this, I feel I am being defined as passive. Like David Jackson (1990) following his heart attack, and many other men, my physical breakdown is a terrifying experience for me because it connects the masculine body with weakness, dependency and passivity. These are the very same 'feminine' qualities that, for years, I have been socialised into defining and defending myself against.

The Elite Performing Body. Early Scripts

The moments from my diary in 1994 that reveal my feelings about my body during that period can usefully be compared to a different body-self I had as a youngster until I was 20 years of age. Unfortunately, I cannot remember this body, I simply cannot recall it. Yet I know it must have existed because of what others have told me and written about it. In terms of the textually created body, the following are extracts from my school magazine and newspaper articles that illustrate the emergence of an elite performing body that was consumed and objectified by others.

In 1968 I was 12 years of age and a member of the unbeaten U13 XV rugby team. The school magazine noted in the first public statement about my body, "This has been a very successful and enjoyable season in many ways (...) Sparkes has been outstanding in the centre." Things developed well. When I was 14 years of age, in 1970, I captained the unbeaten U15 XV. The school magazine commented:

What a truly magnificent season it has been. Unbeaten after twelve games, this has been without question the finest team I have ever had the privilege of coaching. From the start we knew we had in Sparkes a player of outstanding ability and great potential. But although the side was clearly built around his skills, our success has been *entirely* on teamwork (...) This allowed Sparkes at stand-off the change do display the full range of his skills. He delighted us with his strong, penetrating runs, his 32 tries, his crunching tackles, his touch-line conversions and his long relieving kicks out of defence. In addition he has now learnt to vary his play and feed the rest of the line (...) the remarkable team spirit and the superb captaincy of Sparkes have all been factors in this season's story.

In 1972 I captained the 1st XV to one of their best ever seasons. The school magazine described my character as follows:

Without doubt the success of the side has stemmed from his inspiring leadership. His changes of speed, combined with swerve or side-step, have made him a most dangerous attacking player. He has carried out his duties as captain with real efficiency, insisting on a high standard of fitness, and keeping a firm hold on the tactical situation.

The sporting hero story line continues with me making my first class rugby debut early in 1973 for the Bath 1st XV against their arch west-country rivals Gloucester. One newspaper reported the game with the headlines "Andy Sparkes makes a bright start". Another report led with.

> King Edward's School Captain, followed in the illustrious footsteps of Geoff Frankom (a former international) when he made his debut for Bath at Gloucester last week. And a very encouraging start it was too, for this well-built 17-year-old centre in front of what is notoriously one of the most partisan crowds in the country (...) Sparkes not only gave a competent all-round display, but scored half of Bath's points by kicking two penalties and a conversion.

Other newspaper reports included phrases such as "Bath's 17-year-old kicker, Sparkes, made a superb debut." "It was a memorable debut for a young Bath centre, Sparkes, who is not yet 18. He distinguished himself by converting one of Bath's two tries and adding two penalty goals."

Besides these 'Winter tales' there were also early signs of a performing 'Summer body' when I displayed a talent for athletics. For example, in September 1968 the school magazine noted:

> The outstanding athlete this term, however, has been a junior, A.C. Sparkes. In the School Sports he set up new records in the 220 yards, Discus, Shot and Javelin, and in the last event he went on to come first in the North East Somerset Junior Athletics Meeting in Radstock with a throw of 122 ft 6 ins. This beat the existing record by over 20 ft.

The next year I won the South West of England Championships in the javelin with a throw that qualified for the English Schools Athletic Association National Standard of 46 metres. That summer I represented Somerset at the ESAA Annual Championship. I came 6th in the country.

Working-Class Insecurities and the Body

As I write the aching in my back takes my thoughts away from my former body. I think back to my life in school off the playing field. These are not documented so well, but I remember the nagging feelings of insecurity and of not fitting in. These feelings are directly linked to how I located and came to understand myself and my body during those years, and feed into me as I am today.

My mother comes from Gypsy stock and my father comes from a working-class background. The Gypsy link and the working-class roots have formed a strong point of reference in my life, as has the sporting dimension that my father brought into my world. Like many working-class boys, I quickly learned that certain forms of body work were appropriate. I don't remember much about my childhood, but I do remember my Gypsy grandfather teaching me to box and going to watch my Father play football. I do remember him rolling a ball to me on both sides so that I learned to kick with both feet. I remember that connections with him were always associated with the body in action. As I grew up and my sporting talent became visible, he would drive me to rugby and football matches or athletic meetings. He gained pleasure from my performances, and I gained pleasure from pleasing him. Perhaps, as Mark Simpson (1993) points out, sport is one of the few arenas where males (particularly those from the working-classes) can express their love for each other and talk about the body in specific ways.

During the acute phases of my back problem prior to both operations my 71-year-old father became my official taxi-driver, which involved a 350-mile journey each time on his part. In the car, we have created space to talk to each other in ways that don't happen on a 'normal' regular basis since he and Mum got divorced and Dad moved in with his new partner. The talk always referred to the performing body; about my father's talented body and what he'd done when he was younger, what I'd done, and what my brother was doing now in his rugby. The performing, material body and not feelings and emotions were what got talked about. The confusions, anxieties, and fears that haunted me about who I was and what the future held for me in corporeal terms were sidestepped; we moved around them but not near them. For my part, I didn't ask my dad about the emotions he must be going through. Those were not the kind of questions you asked him. There were times in the car when I just wanted him to say 'I love you'. I knew he did, in his terms, from how he had acted and supported me throughout my life. I just wanted it verbalised. Instead, we spoke of bodies.

My father was born in 1924 into a working-class family and grew up without a male presence in the house. His own Dad died when he was just 2 years old from pneumonia with lungs weakened from gassing during World War I. He was clearly a very talented sportsman. Indeed, he almost left the shoe factory where he worked on leaving school as a cutter to become a professional soccer player. Equally as clear was that, with no father around, sport for him was a means of proving himself in masculine terms.

I glance out of my office to a wall where an old, black-and-white, picture of a football team is framed. My father, in his early 20s, is in the centre of second row. The front of his shirt is undone revealing the top of a muscular chest and a sinewy neck. He is solidly built with broad shoulders and black curly hair. He looks lean and fit. I then notice that the whole of the second row are standing on a step. That explains their 'height'. My father was only about 5 ft 9 inches but often played centre-half, a defensive position, against much bigger opponents. I know from what people and his own collection of newspaper cuttings have told me, that he could handle them due to his own physical strength and high skill levels with the ball. He seemed most at home, however, in creative midfield roles. Even as I look, I feel and know another image in the picture, a frame behind the frame, I look and know that my father feels insecure with all that surrounds him. I know that in this picture, like many others, the display is about boarding up an insecure sense of self – a self that over the years has been prone to deep bouts of depression. I know because I have seen myself, and lived moments, in similar photographs.

Up until the age of 11, I attended a local primary school. Here, I guess I must have been defined as reasonably bright. I was conscientious, worked hard, and was made Head Boy in my final year. It was during this year that I took, and passed, the public examination known as the 11+. The significance of this examination is difficult to underestimate for the children of that period in England, and particularly for those from the working classes. Passing, meant you gained a place in a grammar school where academic work was emphasised along with the chance of upward mobility in the social order. Failing, meant going to a secondary modern school that was geared more towards 'practical' subjects and the production of blue collar workers. Being aware of the precarious nature of this lottery, coupled with the belief in a good education as a means of getting on in life, my father had also arranged for me to sit the entrance exam for the local fee-paying, all boys, direct-grant school where the academic standards were very high. I passed, and got in. My parents were really proud of me. As my friends from primary school went one way, mainly to the secondary modern school, I went another into a world that was strange to me. A world that was to reinforce my insecure self – a working-class boy in a middle/upper class school.

King's school was definitely 'posh' to me. Many of those in my class had come from the school's own Junior section and knew each other. Many spoke with posh accents, had fathers who were doctors, solicitors and so on. All this intimidated me; I felt alienated and was often made to feel that I didn't belong by some of the other pupils. Any friendships that did emerge tended to be with those boys who found themselves in a similar position to me. Perhaps they, like me, experienced the anguish of feeling intellectually inferior and 'stupid' in many school subjects. Insidiously, this school environment worked on me so that by the time I passed my 6 'O' levels at the age of 16 and entered the 6th form, I didn't believe I had much to offer academically. However, as I indicated earlier my performing body was making a statement for me. On the rugby field it didn't matter what your parents did of where you lived. The games field was my zone of security where I was a somebody to be reckoned with. Not surprisingly, during my school career a core strand of my sense of self was defined as a sports performer and my performances physically defined me. My body, not my mind, delivered the goods. Descartes would have been proud of me!

Joining Elite Bodies

Pupils at King's School were expected to get at least three Advanced Level examination passes prior to going onto university and then into the 'professions'. I managed to pass Biology at Advanced Level. Clearly, not university material but OK for a college education. My PE teacher at King's and coach of the rugby 1st XV had gone to Loughborough Colleges, an elite, all-male institution specialising in the training of physical education teachers. He suggested I apply there. I did, and they offered me a place to begin in September 1973. On arrival, I immediately got into the 1st XV rugby, something of a rarity given the stiff opposition for places and the quality of the teams that Loughborough ran in those days. The programme for the 1974 Loughborough Colleges versus St Luke's College (Exeter), our major rivals, included all the squad members for both teams. Next to my photograph were the words: "Wing/centre. Age 18. Height 6ft. Weight 13st 4lb. The only freshman to play in the first team back division this year. The youngest of the squad, he played for Bath and Somerset U 19's before entering college. First year PE and Biology. Home Club: Bath."

It was during this year that what I have come to call the 'fatal flaw' revealed itself. Even at 6 feet and 186 lbs I had always felt small and lacking in strength compared to other players in the rugby team, at Bath and at Loughborough. Fast and skilful, for sure, but in my eyes I lacked upper body strength and power. So, toward the end of the spring term, I began to find myself spending more and more time in the weights room. By the start of the summer term I was weight-training on a regular basis and there were clear signs of progress. As a meso-morph I was putting on muscle, and I felt good about this. I saw a difference in my own body, and the changes were noted by others. It was here that the fatal flaw came into my life. I was in the weights room working toward the end of a session when I did my 'legs', that is, deep squats with heavy weights on my back and then leg-press on the multi-gym. It was a hot day and I remember the sweat dripping off the end of my nose and onto my thighs as I sat down on the leg-press machine. Having adjusted the location of the seat and set the weight stack where I wanted it, I completed two sets of 15 reps. I rested, then upped the weight and returned for my third set. As I pushed my legs into the extended position, I felt, and heard, a small click in my lower back. No pain, just a 'click' and the feeling of something tearing slightly. That, for me, was when it began.

Working the Body Shell

Once the Fatal Flaw had revealed itself, a specific trajectory was invoked upon my life. This began during the summer vacation I was examined by an orthopaedic surgeon. Following a brief inspection of my back, a quick look at the X-rays, a few side bends, and a few prods, he told me that my first-class sporting career was over. When he said this, I felt nothing, just a numbness. Then I felt a wave of hatred for this man and his arrogance at dismissing my dreams in such a matter-of-fact way. I just wanted to get out of the room. I remember walking down the corridor to the out-patients reception area to ring my father for a lift home. I didn't tell him what had been said, but once I had put the phone down I began to cry in the phone booth. From that moment on I bottled my emotions up about my 'back problem'.

Things were bad enough medically for my college to give me a year off. During this time I had various treatments from orthopaedic surgeons which included having my upper body in a plaster cast for 6 weeks, and several epidural injections. None of this worked and, following some osteopathic treatment, I eventually ended up doing a 6-week stint at a rehabilitation centre near London that specialised in sports injuries. This intense period of treatment that built up the muscles around my lumbar spine and reeducated them to support me appropriately got me going again in a bodily sense, and I returned to college.

Returning to college was strange – down a year, in with a new bunch of PE students (jocks) who were suspicious of me due to the reputation I had left with. I couldn't do things like gymnastics and some of the athletics, but overall I had grasped back some of my performing body so that, in combination with an emerging 'academic' mind, I ended up as 'top jock' in that second year. I can't remember how I felt when I saw the list go up at the end of the year. It must have made some impact because after it had been up a while, I stole it from the board. I only found it recently in my 'scrap box' when I began to write this paper. There it was, in black and white, the Year 2 combined practical and theory results of July 1976. No 1, Sparkes A. 80.91; No 2 Smith R. A. 76.10.

Despite this apparent return to 'glory days', I didn't feel part of what was going on. Perhaps, deep down inside, I never really did. My introverted nature did not sit well with the cultivated extroversion and machismo that characterised the dominant jock culture. My sense of self had begun to shift, and I found solitude in a certain detachment from what was going on. I had always read widely, but now I was into reading literature in a big way. *The Glass Bead Game* by Herman Hesse (1969), for example, made a big impact on me. All this was rather strange to my PE colleagues. Perhaps I was already attempting to redefine myself towards a more intellectual me, a 'forgotten' me, a me that was not predominantly defined by a performing body. After all I knew mine was 'flawed'. This is not to suggest that I did not get involved in various sports. However, my main focus was on keeping myself fit, and I was spending more and more time in the weights room building up the outer shell of my body as a mode of protection, to keep the fatal flaw at bay, and to shore up an unstable and insecure sense of self.

On leaving university I got a job teaching for several years. It was a relatively pain-free time with only a couple of acute episodes with my back that were relieved by manipulation. I played some competitive sport in the local football league but didn't take it too seriously. As before, I was keeping myself really fit. I ran every day. The school also had a set of free-weights which allowed me to continue working on my body shell. Over time this shell got to look very chiseled and defined. I looked a performer and the shell gave me some security, especially as PE teacher. But my muscular body in this role also exacerbated a tension that continually confronted me. This involved the stereotypical view held in educational circles, and society at large, that to be sporting and teach a 'practical' subject like PE meant that the person had few intellectual capabilities. The very body that I was constructing to protect one aspect of my identity was creating the opposite effect in terms of developing and sustaining another key identity to my sense of self.

Partly because of these tensions, I left teaching and paid my own way through a master's degree. Then it was back into teaching for a couple of years. More gym work and more serious now, I joined a tough local gym that prided itself on no-nonsense approach to training and its population of hard-core bodybuilders. Now it was split body routines, super-sets, and forced-reps. Of course, deep leg squats were out, so I was limited on my leg work. However, I watched myself grow and tone up. As a mesomorph I had a lot of advantages, and some of the hardcore expressed envy at my low body fat and ability to gain muscle. This muscle was often put to good use in the martial arts classes that I attended on a regular basis. I looked very fit, and moved, for most of the time, in accordance with the image my body displayed. Yet, during this period, the fatal flaw began to appear again on a more regular basis. There was a certain irony in me seeming to take greater control of my body just as the flaw began to reassert its right to disrupt my life. This visible loss of control over the body struck at the heart of me. It shattered the facade I put up.

I particularly hated those days when, as a PE teacher, I was hobbling about. The pupils didn't know what to make of it. After all there were no visible injuries, nothing broken, and wasn't this same teacher bounding around with us yesterday? They were bemused by the sight of my muscular frame twisted by an invisible hand. This coupled with, once again, my hostility to how I felt people perceived me as a PE teacher – that is, stupid – led me resign from teaching several more times before registering for my Ph.D. on a part-time basis while I was employed as a taxi driver.

By now I had decided that I did not want to go back into teaching in schools. Deep down inside, I think I knew that my body would not take the physical strain of acting out such a role. Luckily, in 1984 I gained a lecturing position in physical education & sports science back at, what had now become, Loughborough University. Once again, I was surrounded by elite performing bodies. Once again, I came into daily contact with the notions of perfectible and disciplined bodies that could be shaped by training regimes based on sound scientific principles. Amid this sea of controlled bodies, my own fatal flaw was becoming increasingly uncontrollable. Bending to put air in my car tyre, or putting my leg over the arm of a chair, could send my back into spasm, and several days of acute pain would follow. Other days were fine, and I could train hard – manipulations by osteopaths and chiropractors, sclerosing injections, going to the gym to work out around the flaw, to build the shell to protect me from who I was and who I wasn't. This became an embodied cycle of events that increasingly shaped my life.

When my contract at Loughborough finished, I got a job at Exeter University, Loughborough's big rivals for many years in interuniversity sport – from one elite body culture to another. Perhaps not the best place to come to terms with the consequences of the fatal flaw, yet, in other ways, it was the perfect setting to reflect upon the mirror images of my youthful self that I saw before me each day. As part of these reflections I think of the narrative of self provided by Sam Fussell (1991) in his book *Muscle: Confessions of an Unlikely Bodybuilder.* In the opening chapter called 'The Genesis', he describes how during an anxiety attack in 1984 while he was in New York, he ran into a bookshop to hide. Here, he stumbled across *Arnold: The Education of a Bodybuilder* by Arnold Schwarzenegger. A glimpse of the cover, which showed Schwarzenegger posing on a mountain top told him all he needed to know in terms of how the outer body could protect someone from a multitude of fears.

After 4 years devoted to bodybuilding that took over his life and led him to reject and be rejected by his family and friends and to take enormous doses of steroids and other drugs, as he put on 80 pounds of muscle, Fussell (1991) writes in the the final chapter called 'The Aftermath'.

> But this shell that I created wasn't meant just to keep people at bay. After all, a can of Mace could do that. No, this carapace was laboriously constructed to keep things inside too. The physical palisades and escarpments of my body served as a rocky boundary that permitted no passage, no hint of a deeper self – a self I couldn't bear. It wasn't that I was worse than other people. It was that I was just as bad, just as frightened, just as mean, just as angry, and I hated myself for it. Every sin that had a name, I saw in me (...) My deepest fear was that I didn't matter (...) I needed whatever buoy or marker or myth I could find to keep myself from feeling meaningless in the face of infinity. (Fussell 1991, 248)

As I read Fussell's words again I begin to feel uncomfortable. I recognise the socially learned undervaluing of myself that David Jackson (1990) talks about, and the class-based fears and anxieties about my adequacy and credentials to do what I am doing. Like him, I have, and am haunted by, the belief that one day people will find me out as an impostor and fling me out.

No Conclusion. No Happy Ending

In surgical terms my operations in 1988 and 1994 were successful. The prolapsed discs removed from my L3/L4 and L4/L5 lumbar spine now reside in two bottles of preservative on a bathroom shelf. On good days I walk or cycle the 7-mile round trip from my house to work. At this point, it would be good to report that having recognised the limitations in my narrative resourcing, I have been able to find others that have dramatically changed my life and how I interpret and react to events around me. It would be satisfying to report in Athur

Frank's (1994) terms that a new sense of self has arisen ph
out of my experiences. As part of this process I would have
a more communicative relationship with my body. Here, the essential
quality would be that my body has become one that is in the process of
creating itself in a situation where my body's contingency is no longer
its problem but its possibility. Constructing a 'communicative body'
would offer powerful challenges to my former/remaining attachments
to a 'disciplined/obedient' and 'mirroring' body. I have and I haven't.
I'd like to, I'm trying but I'm unsure.

I'd also like to report, following Thomas Gerschick and Adam Miller
(1995, 267), that via my experiences I have been able to wholeheart-
edly reject hegemonic masculinity and develop new standards of masculinity in its place or, at the very least, reformulate an idealised masculinity in terms of my own abilities, perceptions, and strengths so as to
judge my 'manhood' along new lines. I have and I haven't. I'd like to,
I'm trying but I'm unsure. Unfortunately, I all too often relapse into a
reliance that involves a concern with others' views of my masculinity
as I continue to internalise "many more of the ideals of predominant
masculinity, including physical strength, athleticism, independence, and
sexual prowess".

At different times I can locate bits of myself in all the categories
that have just been described. I am sometimes each of all of these, and
more, as change and sameness mix in the same breath. Yet, as Arthur
Frank (1994, 49) has pointed out in his analysis of the rhetoric of
self-change, I simultaneously need these boxes in order to reject them,
"You must change your life, but understand that you will never be
changing in conditions of your own choosing. There are no boxes only
for those who understand what boxes are there." I am learning much
about this statement as I seek to actively increase my narrative resources
in a variety of domains, and in a variety of ways, some of which are
contained in the writing of this paper. In seeking, I find that new narratives of the body are in the making, and that with the end of one
kind of body comes the beginning of other kinds. I remain unsure as
to where that leaves me.

The chronic back problem remains. Intense physical training is out,
as are the kinds of sporting activity normally undertaken by many men
in their early 40s. Yet, deep inside, I still want to push myself in the
domain of intense physical activity and experience the elation it can

sometimes produce. If I do push myself too hard physically the fatal flaw visits me again, my lower back goes into spasm, and I experience pain. Sometimes, it just seems to visit for fun. In short, there is no rhyme or reason, no pattern, to how the fatal flaw works itself in and through my life. Even as I write these words in March 1999, the dull pain in my lower back I get from sitting for long periods deflects my concentration. It has been a bad couple of weeks and I wait for my manipulation with the osteopath in a few days time to try and get me out of yet another acute phase with the fatal flaw. I'm also seeing a physiotherapist who is trying to find ways to re-educate my muscles and improve my posture.

As a consequence, I am not sure how to end this story. Like Carolyn Ellis (1995, 162) I have to request that you the reader, "exist for a time within uncertainty, where plot lines circle round and round, where endings are multiple and often unfinished, and where selves are fractured and often contradictory." Also, like Leslie Bloom and Petra Munro (1995), I want my text to resist an authoritative final interpretation and so I have drenched my story in ambiguity, rejecting the all too tempting desire to place the fragments of my story into a coherent and totalising narrative structure.

In producing a fragmented and, I hope, emotionally charged narrative of self, I have resisted my academic training. This training would have led me to leave the personal story behind and return to distant and detached theory in order to create a sanitised and neat conclusion/resolution to the dilemmas signalled in my story. As a 'wounded storyteller' (Frank 1995), I now treat attempts at this kind of closure with suspicion, as the return to theory deflects my attention away from the very vulnerabilities and fragilities that I need to embrace. The words of David Jackson (1990) echo in my head.

That is why, at times of maximum insecurity (around difficult, unfamiliar ideas), I have a tendency to hide away behind the relative safety of established interpretation, borrowed voices and quotation... it is actually very defensive. The quotations and borrowed voices work like life jackets in a choppy sea, offering points of reassurance in a strangely disorientating arena (...) I often reach for a distancing language when the emotional confrontation is too immediately pain-

ful or confusing. (Jackson 1990, 10)
A return to theory would also be symptomatic of the lack of trust I usually have in my own stories in relation to my own lived experience. My insecurities often lead me to write, in Thomas Barone's (1995) terms, as a declarative author-persuader rather than an artful writer-persuader. The former seeks direct control over the interpretations placed upon the text in the act of reading. In contrast, the latter understands the necessity of relinquishing control, of trusting the readers and allowing them the freedom to interpret and evaluate the text from their unique vantage points so that they can contribute answers to the dilemmas posed. I choose to trust you. Please make your own contribution to my story.

Acknowledgements

This chapter is a substantially shortened, less theoretically elaborate, and more trusting version of paper that originally appeared in Sparkes, A. (1996) The Fatal Flaw: A narrative of the fragile body-self. *Qualitative Inquiry,* 2 (4), 463-494. I am grateful to Sage Publications Ltd for their kind permission to reprint parts of the paper here.

References

Barone, Thomas (1995) Persuasive writings, vigilant readings, and reconstructed characters: The paradox of trust in educational storysharing. In A. Hatch & R. Wisniewski (Eds.) *Life History and Narrative.* London: Falmer Press, 62-74.

Bloom, Leslie Rebecca & Munro Petra (1995) Conflicts of selves: Nonunitary subjectivity in women administrators' life history narratives. In A. Hatch & R. Wisniewski (Eds.) *Life History and Narrative.* London: Falmer Press, 99-112.

Connell, Robert (1995) *Masculinities.* Cambridge: Polity Press.

Ellis, Carolyn (1995) On the other side of the fence: Seeing black and white in a small town. *Qualitative Inquiry,* 1 (2), 147-167.

Frank, Arthur (1994) The rhetoric of self-change: Illness experience as narrative. *The Sociological Quarterly,* 34 (1), 39-52.

Frank, Arthur (1995) *The Wounded Storyteller*. Chicago: University of Chicago Press.

Fussell, Sam (1991) *Muscle: Confessions of an Unlikely Bodybuilder*. London: Scribners.

Gerschick, T. J. & Miller, A. S. (1995) Coming to terms: Masculinity and physical disability: In: D. Sabo & D Gordon (Eds), *Men's Health and Illness*. London: Sage.

Healy, John (1988) *The Grass Arena*. London: Faber & Faber.

Hesse, Hermann (1969) *The Glass Bead Game*. London: Holt, Rinehart and Winston.

Jackson, David (1990) *Unmasking Masculinity: A Critical Autobiography*. London: Unwin Hyman.

Simpson, Mark (1993) *Male Impersonators: Men Performing Masculinity*. London: Cassell.

David Jackson

A COCK-SURE BODY

All those Grammar school years it took me
to build and hold together the make-believe
of a cock-sure body.

At work, I threw out what I had for a chest,
grew a straggly moustache, clamping my ribs
and buttocks, firm and tight.

At conferences I struck sparks off the platform
from the empty thunder of my cowboy boots.

But it only took eight, short minutes
to lose a grip on who
I thought I was.

In eight minutes' flat I was unmanned.
Lost my cowboy strut in the spinning
eye of the whirlpool. My sureness buckled
as my knees caved in. Had peed myself in fear.

It was only then that
I could move back against those hardening years
through my fortress, crumbling.

Andrew C. Sparkes & Brett Smith

DISRUPTED SELVES AND NARRATIVE RECONSTRUCTIONS

Introduction

Sport, and in particular contact sports, have long been associated with the construction and maintenance of specific forms of embodied, hegemonic masculinity (Curry 1993; Hickey, Fitzclarence and Matthews 1998; Messner 1992; Messner and Sabo 1990; Sparkes 1996; Thornton 1993). As Harris (1995) notes, becoming an athlete can be a crucial masculinizing experience that engenders a self-confidence which generalizes to all aspects of a man's life. Accordingly, Connell (1995) indicates how in, a context where masculinity is almost always thought to proceed from men's bodies, sport has come to be the leading definer of masculinity in mass culture by providing a continuous display of men's bodies in motion. However, and significant for our interests in this chapter, Connell went on to suggest that "The constitution of masculinity through bodily performance means that gender is vulnerable when the performance cannot be sustained – for instance, as a result of physical disability" (ibid. 54).

Gerschick and Miller (1995, 183) suggest that the body is often the "central foundation of how men define themselves and how they are defined by others". If this is so, what then of men who have developed their bodies through sport, have successfully negotiated a specific male identity and had it validated through a specific sport, but then experience a spinal cord injury (SCI) playing the very sport that has contributed so much to this process? After all, SCIs are traumatic life events that are immensely disruptive to a person's life story (Kleiber, Brock, Lee, Dattilo, and Caldwell 1995; Seymour 1998). These traumas are likely to be accentuated for those individuals described by Brock and Kleiber (1994), who shape their life narrative significantly around the body's performance in sport. This is because although any future self imaginable has a body, the importance of that body will vary greatly from one life story to the next.

At a general level Shakespeare, Gillespie-Sells, and Davies (1996), remind us of the pervasive assumption that disability and masculinity are conflicting identities because of the ostensible contradiction contained in the stereotypical visions of each. At a more local and personalised level, Murphy (1990, 94) notes in writing of his own experiences with disability: "Paralytic disability constitutes emasculation of a more direct and total nature. For the male, the weakening and atrophy of the body threaten all the cultural values of masculinity: strength, activeness, speed, virility, stamina, and fortitude."

Given the views of Shakespeare et al. (1996), and Murphy (1990), we were surprised to learn, in our attempt to develop our thinking in relation to the connections between sport, bodies, masculinities, and disability, that there has been little empirical research on men and masculinities. We were even more surprised to learn from Shakespeare et al. (1996), that there has been even less empirical research on men, masculinities, and disability. A rare exception to this rule, however, being Gerschick and Miller's (1995) small study of men with disabilities.

Gerschick and Miller (1995), suggested there were three dominant identity patterns that men with physical disabilities used to cope with their situations. They called them the three Rs: reformulation, which entailed men redefining standards of hegemonic characteristics on their own terms; reliance, which entailed men internalising the contemporary aspects of hegemonic masculinity and attempting to meet these standards; and in some cases rejection, which was characterised by the renunciation of hegemonic standards and was about creating alternative masculine identities and subcultures.

Another exception would be the work of Seymour (1998), whose study illustrates the threat that disability poses to hegemonic forms of masculinity with regard to appearance and body image; social routines and relationships; involvement with disabled sports; intimate activities; and bodily continence.

It remains, however, an unsettling fact that there is a serious lack of research which focuses on the embodied experiences of men who have acquired a disability through sport.

Participants and Methodology

According to Nauright and Chandler (1996) the game of rugby union football, particularly in the United Kingdom, has been viewed as one of the most masculine and manly of sports. It has been noted how rugby union was, and remains, largely a male preserve which constructs, and sustains, a subculture that sanctions and glorifies aggression, violence, control, discipline, force, homophobia, heterosexism, and the subordination of 'others' as expressions of a dominant hegemonic masculinity. The four men we focus upon in this chapter have all been heavily involved in this sport, have experienced a C-4/5 SCI through playing rugby, and now define themselves as disabled.

Mark (all participants have been ascribed pseudonyms), and Richard, are in their mid-thirties, Matthew is in his early-forties, and Eamonn in his mid-twenties. All are white, born in the United Kingdom and are currently unemployed. All the participants were highly committed to sport before SCI. In particular, Matthew, Mark and Eamonn had played county standard rugby union. Richard, progressed as far as the England U19 level in this sport, as well as boxing at England school boy level. Consequently, all the participants had cultivated a sporting, disciplined body and developed a strong athletic identity (Brewer, Van Raalte, and Linder 1993; Frank 1995; Sparkes 1996, 1998).

As part of a larger study, initial contact was made with the participants via the English Rugby Football Union's (RFU) support network for injured players[1]. In accordance with ethical procedures, we did not seek or desire to know the identity of any members of this group. To ensure confidentiality, and following negotiations with the Sports Injuries Administrator for this organisation, it was agreed that an open letter from ourselves explaining the project, along with a brief questionnaire seeking demographic details, would be distributed in one of the series of newsletters circulated by the support network for the injured players. The questionnaire ended by asking the respondent to indicate if they would agree to be interviewed about their experiences, and if so to provide their name and address in a stamped addressed envelope that was also supplied. Following this, forty men who have experienced spinal cord injuries through playing rugby union agreed to be interviewed.

Our study is informed by the principles of interpretive interactionism, and interpretive biography, as developed by Denzin (1989a, 1989b). Accordingly, Matthew, Mark, Richard, and Eamonn were involved in confidential, thematic, informal, life history interviews conducted in their homes by Brett Smith, who acted as an 'active listener' (Wolcott 1995), in an attempt to assist the participants tell their life story in their own way and in their own words. Each participant was interviewed at least twice, with each interview lasting between two and five hours. All interviews were tape-recorded, transcribed, and analysed thematically and reflexively, adopting a posture of indwelling as described by Maykut and Morehouse (1994), and drawing on Wolcott's (1994) thoughts on description, analysis, and interpretation.

The Body as an Absent Presence

Prior to SCI, Matthew, Mark, Richard, and Eamonn, not uncommonly, took their bodies for granted. In Gadow's (1982) terms, the body is most often experienced in a state of 'primary immediacy'. This is a state of being, when the body functions and performs tasks without conscious effort, and there is an overriding unity between body and self. Indeed, Leder (1990) argues, that the body disappears from consciousness when it is functioning in this non-problematic state. Quite simply, the body becomes an absent presence.

Talking of his body pre-SCI, Richard comments, "Looking back its quite strange. You use it [the body] all the time and, for me, more than most people because of my past job [as a fireman] and since, I suppose, because I played a lot of sport. You just don't think about it [the body], well not until becoming disabled". Likewise, Matthew noted: "Obviously, you don't think about things. Your body and everything just click into place. It's not really something you think about, even

79

though you always used it". Finally, in summarizing the situation, Eamonn said: "But like most things when you are able-bodied you just don't think about it, you just do it".

Through their sporting involvement in rugby football union, the participants also cultivated this sense of primary immediacy through the process of engagement with developmentally challenging activities in which a new unity of self and body are readily imagined and achieved (Sparkes 1998). Once achieved, this *cultivated immediacy* is characteristic of the enjoyment-orientated self-expression, and the feelings of 'flow', experienced in sporting situations where the consciousness of self disappears as ability matches challenges and action merges with awareness (Csikszentmihalyi 1993). For these men, sport largely cultivated this sense of primary immediacy so that in specific activities a body-self unity was maintained (Kleiber et al. 1995). As Eamonn stated: "When you were playing [sport], it reminds me of what American runners called being 'in the zone'. For me, nothing mattered, bothered you that is, when you where on the pitch".

Specific forms of masculinity were also developed over time in relation to the participants' experiences of cultivated immediacy through sport. As the following comments by Matthew and Richard indicate, the performing body and its connectedness to masculinity formed an absent presence in the lives of these men prior to SCI.

Sport and being a man go together. Just look at school, all the kids who couldn't play sport, proper sport, – not girls sport, I mean, – got picked on, bullied or from what I can remember, were not as popular as the guys who played rugby and football...I don't think you realised these parts though, you just played sport mainly for fun and everything seemed to follow...You never thought about the masculine thing anyway, because you knew you were stronger, in control, and fitter than most people. In one sense it just came with the territory. (Matthew)

I don't think that I really thought about being a man. But, its still important, very. I mean, when I think about it, and I do, I typified being a proper man – playing sport, women, drinking. I mean you had to be in the team I used to play in. If you didn't play rugby, or anything like it, we thought they were gay or something. (Richard)

These comments by Richard and Matthew, reveal the manner in which athletic identities, coupled with a specific form of masculinity, are developed via contact sports. They also reveal how closely this is connected with expressions of hegemonic masculinity that, according to Messner (1997), partly constructs itself relationally by marginalizing and subordinating various 'others', such as, women, gay men, and people with disabilities. The inherent sexism, heterosexism, homophobia, and able-bodyism in the previous comments are symptomatic of these issues with regard to rugby football and other contact sports. All of this was embodied and taken-for-granted by Matthew, Mark, Richard, and Eamonn who were secure with particular ways of being a 'sporting man'.

Spinal Cord Injury. Disrupted Body-Self

Spinal cord injury, as form of 'biographical disruption' (Bury 1982), shakes earlier taken-for-granted assumptions about possessing a smoothly functioning body, and drastically disrupts any sense of body-self unity. Paradoxically, following SCI, the body becomes dis-harmonious from the self and inescapably embodied (Toombs 1992). It is now experienced as an oppositional force which becomes prob-lematic and dys-appears. Here, as Frank (1998) notes, body dys-appearence is not only appearance as dysfunction; it also denotes loss. This loss is associated with the immediate loss of primary and cultivated immediacy which is now experienced as a disrupted immediacy that threatens a number of 'core' identities. As Eamonn and Mark com-mented:

> The body is so important to who I am, who we are perceived as, and because of the accident, you can't do the things that you love and which make who we are as a person. Sport, rugby, the feelings of being lost in yourself, you just can't replicate them in some test tube. I've lost those feelings which, I suppose, are like a drug in a sense. I still crave for those experiences and feelings. (Eamonn)

Everything now is like chalk is to cheese. These opposites hit you really hard and I'm unsure if I will ever come to terms with these contrasts. When I look in the mirror, I see this broken body, and then I kind of see my body that was supremely fit and muscular. You start thinking about the things which were important, like rugby, that you can't do now. I miss that, the physical, the adrenaline pumping, the 'buzz'. Yeah, those feelings which you only really get from sport. (Mark)

Matthew, Mark, Craig, and Eamonn further suggested that the biographical disruption caused by SCI led to devalued notions of themselves as people. This was partly due to the rapid dissolution of two central aspects of their sense of self.

Shattered Masculinities

Following a SCI, many men find that their previous masculine sense of self as dominant, assertive, and aggressive becomes problematic. For Mark, his masculine sense of self has been lost, "After the accident, your masculinity does tend to go (...) Bang! Something which is important to you has literally been shattered". Echoing these sentiments, Eamonn notes, "Your masculinity is gone, broken. You just struggle to live up to it [masculinity]". Likewise, Matthew commented, "In this sense, 'feeling like a man' almost evaporates (...) If you have been masculine in the past, you forget that after a point, from a physical side, your masculinity is gone." Finally, Richard stated:

Because you don't really class yourself as the dominant masculine male, that normally goes out, earns the money and be the bread-winner, does the decorating, do the gardening, sort the children out, and do everything. Then all of a sudden, you are sat in a wheelchair and you can't do any of those things. You are totally the opposite...It really takes some coming to terms with, some getting used to, even though you, in a way, you have lost your masculinity. In this respect, its probably, for me anyway, one of the biggest shocks that you have to face when you become disabled.

The Loss of Athletic Identity

Associated with, and intimately connected to, the loss of specific masculine identities for Matthew, Mark, Richard, and Eamonn was the loss of their personal, social, and physical, athletic identities[2]. As Mark commented:

> I think, because rugby played an important part in my life, not only the playing but socialising as well, people recognised me as sportsman. It was a big part of my life, and your friends are from the [rugby] club. So, of course, you come to think of yourself as a sportsman – even though you know you are not going to play for England or anything (...) Now, well, I miss that side of my life. I miss being a sportsman and everything that goes with it. It was a big part of me. Now, because of the injury, I'm really a no-one, not who I really am.

Echoing these feelings, Matthew noted:

> Sport was essentially my life. I was studying sport at college, playing rugby at a high standard, and most of my friends were involved with sport or came from sport. Obviously, when this happens [SCI], you lose a lot of those friends. You miss playing, you miss the game because you've put in so much time, so much of your life. If its really important to you, you're going to miss it.

These comments suggest that an athletic identity is placed close to the apex of a personal, identity hierarchy, for Matthew, Mark, Richard, and Eamonn. As a result, the loss of this identity is extremely difficult to cope with since they are so closely associated with their masculine senses of self. Of course, following rehabilitation, participation in sports for people with disabilities is a possible option. However, the strength of the athletic identity formed via their perception of what constitutes a high level, embodied, and skilled performance, negates the satisfaction that might be gained from involvement in sports for people with disabilities. Disability, for Eamonn: "Does take the enjoyment away from the sport because you are not just participating in the sport. You are fighting your body, and you have to rely on aids and adaptations to take part in that sport." Similarly, Richard noted: "How can you play sports like that? I mean, I can understand people using sport for rehabilitation and everything. For me though, they aren't real sports, not really. Anyway, I never got any satisfaction from disabled sports, not like I did from football or rugby. Before the accident that is".

Such comments show the psychological distance or 'disruption of fit' (Mathieson & Stam 1995), between previous and current senses of self. Here, the 'real me' does 'real sports', and 'disabled sports' for Matthew, Mark, Eamonn, and Richard, no matter how good they become, are currently defined as inferior. This is not an uncommon reaction for men who have previously played sport to a high level and then acquire a disability. As Seymour (1998, 115) pointed out, "Success in disabled, unlike success in able-bodied sport, is not associated with mastery in other dimensions of life (...) Disabled sport remains sport for people with damaged bodies." Hence, involvement in sports for people with disabilities can have a negative effect for some, since it constantly reminds the performer of what they were or used to be. For such men, as Seymour suggests, sport may impede rather than facilitate reembodiment and so sport as a form of rehabilitation to promote enjoyment, a valued sense of self, and competence might not be useful for all men.

Narrative Refuge and Restored Selves

In the face of what are experienced as major losses, Matthew, Eamonn, Richard, and Mark desire to be what they once were. That is, as a strategy and style, in attempting to reconcile the self or cope with their disability (Bury 1991), they take narrative refuge in what Charmaz (1987) calls a *restored self*.

> The restored self means the identity level in which ill persons expect to return to their former lives. Those pursuing it take it for granted that this is the normal course of events, the natural sequence of even serious illness. People who aim for this identity level not only aim to reconstruct a similar physical self as before, but also to assume continuity with the self before illness. (Charmaz 1987, 287)

The desire for a restored self is reflected in the following comment by

Matthew: "I can't do any of those things I used to really enjoy, like work, play rugby, football, pop out for a drink. That is why I want my old life back. This (a person who is disabled) is not me." For Richard, who has sought restoration via alternative therapies, including four trips to Lourdes with another visit planned in the future, "I hate being quadriplegic and I am still trying for a cure. I still see myself as able bodied and I can't understand anyone who says they wouldn't want to be able bodied, unless you maybe you were born that way [disabled]." Similar views were expressed by Mark and Eamonn.

> I am, although I am not, able-bodied. What I mean, well, I think of myself as more able-bodied than disabled. I have very little in common with most disabled people and that's one reason why I don't socialise with them. Yeah, I do want my old life back. I'm giving it my best shot, so I might get back myself (Mark).

> We live in such an able-bodied world that, of course, you want your old body back. It might sound anti-disabled or something, but I really do hope that I will be able to walk someday, to get back my old life (...) Of course, I want myself back. My body played a big part in defining who I was and, once I get my body back, then (laughs) as Arnold Schwarzenegger would say 'I'll be back'. (Eamonn)

As Charmaz (1994) notes, these comments are typical of many men who attempt to reclaim the same identities, and the same lives, they had before they became impaired or acquired a disability through illness. Clearly, a desire to return to prior body-self relationships is important for Matthew, Mark, Richard, and Eamonn. More specifically, within the types of restored selves identified by Charmaz (1987) they appear to be holding on to an *entrenched self*.

> Restoring an entrenched self means being wedded to a self-conception situated in the past. These persons hold clear images of their self-concepts, which they can readily articulate. The entrenched self represents patterns of action, conviction, and habit built up over the years. These unchanged patterns had been a source of self-respect before illness. After illness, resuming these patterns becomes the person's major objective. (...) Restoring an entrenched self also

has the imagery of a 'comeback'. (Charmaz 1987, 302).

Charmaz (1994) further emphasises, failed attempts to recapture past selves can lead to despondency and invalidism, as all valued social and personal identities remain in the irretrievable past. Moreover, being unable to measure up to the past self results in further preoccupation with it, and heightens identity dilemmas. As the distance increases between their past self (now reconstructed in memory in idealised form) and present identities, the former valued identities collapse and new ones are viewed as negative. Importantly, with each identity loss due to SCI the preservation of valued 'performing' identities becomes increasingly difficult. Thus, for Matthew, Mark, Eamonn, and Richard, the focus on an entrenched self appears to heighten identity dilemmas since the past-self is often considered to represent the 'real self', replaced irrevocably by a new false persona associated with disability. That is, idealised, and a preoccupation with, the past serve as a painful index of what has been lost, and what now had to be 'tolerated' on a daily basis. In this context, feelings of frustration, anger and depression are common (Shakespeare et al. 1994; Sparkes 1996, 1998).

Discussion

Many interpretations can be made of the themes we have focused upon that have emerged in the lives of Matthew, Richard, Eamonn, and Mark. For us, these moments signal the difficulty some men have in reconstructing or restoring a valued sense of self in the face of a traumatic biographical disruption. In part, these difficulties are made worse by the strength of the athletic identities developed by the participants through their involvement in rugby football, and other contact sports, prior to SCI. Likewise, the reinforcement this sport, and other cultural practices they have been involved in, provided for the maintenance and affirmation of hegemonic masculinity also add to the problems of restorying the self.

As the data suggests, despite their demise, hegemonic masculine identities, athletic identities, and an expressive, competent, body-self, are apparently able to maintain their salient position at the apex of Matthew, Mark, Eamonn, and Richard's hierarchy of identities. In combination, this acts to exert pressure on these men to seek a restored self no matter how unrealistic or self-defeating this may be. Indeed, in Gerschick and Miller's (1995) terms, they have primarily chosen reliance over reformulation, or rejection, with regard to views on masculinity:

> We found that many of our informants were concerned with others' views of their masculinity and with meeting the demands of hegemonic masculinity. They primarily used the second pattern, reliance, which involved the internalization of many more of the ideals of predominant masculinity, including physical strength, athleticism, independence, and sexual prowess. (...) As such, these men did not seem to be comfortable with their sense of manhood: indeed, their inability to meet society's standards bothered them very much. (Gerschick and Miller 1995, 191).

Gerschick and Miller (1995) note, that when men with disabilities opt for a reliance strategy they are placed in a double bind situation. This is because, even though they embraced dominant conceptions of masculinity as a way to gain acceptance from themselves and from others, they are also reminded in their interactions with others that they are 'incomplete'. As a consequence, the identities behind the facade suffer, and there are many costs associated with any strategy that adheres to such a narrow definition of masculinity. However, as the words of Matthew, Mark, Eamonn, and Richard suggest, for some sportsmen relinquishing this strategy is an option that is just too costly to contemplate.

Of course, this is to presume that these men have the resources to contemplate options with regard to restorying their lives. We would suggest that this might not be the case. In particular, their opportunities and willingness to reembody, or reconstruct themselves, so as to form a different body-self relationship are, in part, constrained due their elective affinity for what Frank (1995) calls a *restitution narrative*. This is the dominant, or canonical, narrative regarding illness in Western cultures. It has as its basic story line: "Yesterday I was healthy, today I'm sick, but tomorrow I'll be healthy again."

Narratives, like the restitution narrative, as received stories can be constraining. This is because they tend to advocate appropriate or correct behaviour, and thus provide specific versions of the way the world should be. Hence, in defining and prescribing behaviour, these narratives provide a powerful cultural frame through which individuals make sense of their lived experiences. As Frank (1995) recognizes, the basic storyline of the restitution narrative ties in closely with notions of a restorable body. Frank, went on to suggest that even though a belief that the suffering of illness will be relieved is the preferred narrative for any body, some bodies display a greater affinity for restitution narratives than others. This is particularly so, when notions of the restored and disciplined body are invoked, and the teller of the tale wants the body's former predictability back again. In such conditions, Frank (1995) argued:

> The body that turns in upon itself is split from the self that looks forward to this body's restitution. The temporarily broken-down body becomes 'it' to be cured. Thus the self is dissociated from the body. (...) The restitution story is about remaking the body in an image derived either from its own history before illness or elsewhere.(...) In the restitution story, the implicit genesis of illness is an unlucky breakdown in a body that is conceived on mechanistic lines. To be fixable, the body has to be a kind machine. (...) Restitution narratives require fixing, and fixing requires such a mechanistic view. The mechanistic view normalizes illness: televisions require fixing, so do bodies. (Frank 1995, 85-88)

Frank's (1995) thesis that different bodies have *elective affinities* to different narratives would appear to have some relevance to the stories told by Matthew, Mark, Eamonn, and Richard. That is, the kind of body they developed, and operated with, within specific cultural contexts played a key role in creating, and confirming, a set of 'core' identities and a sense of self. This, in turn, led them choose certain storylines over others among those available in the cultural repertoire available to them. These choices, and the manner in which they are embodied, help frame the dilemmas experienced by these men.

Correspondingly, the combined effect of a strong athletic identity, an affinity for hegemonic forms of masculinity and the restitution narrative, diminishes the ability of Matthew, Eamonn, Richard, and Mark to narratively reconstruct their sense of self. These strands work together to reduce their access to, and flexibility to engage with, the wider cultural repertoire of potential stories that are available for synthesis into personal stories. In part, this is exacerbated by their lack of space and opportunity to operate not just as 'survivors' but also to act as 'witness' to their own experiences. As Frank (1995, 137) notes, survival does not include any particular responsibility other than continuing to survive: "Becoming a witness assumes a responsibility for telling what happened. The witness offers testimony to a truth that is generally unrecognized or suppressed. People who tell stories of illness are witnesses, turning illness into moral responsibility." Frank, goes on to emphasise that offering testimony *implicates* others in what they witness, and that "part of what turns stories into testimony is the call made upon another person to receive that testimony" (ibid. 141). As a consequence, witnessing and receiving testimony are not solitary acts but depend upon relationships to activate and sustain them.

Unfortunately for Matthew, Eamonn, Richard, and Mark these relationships have yet to develop and so their stories remain silenced, to themselves and others. The act of witness is absent. This is not unusual in Western cultures in general, and sporting subcultures in particular, where there is a reluctance to hear stories of disability. The preference is for 'Hollywood stories' that glamorize and embrace tales of triumph against the odds, that is, restitution narratives. This fore grounding and legitimising of specific narratives at the expense of others that are marginalized, silenced, or considered as 'negative' may contribute greatly to the problems of restorying the self for those who acquire a disability through sport (Sparkes 1996, 1998).

Having said this, we do not want to suggest that Matthew, Mark, Eamonn, and Richard should be denied the right and the opportunity to attempt to restore a valued sense of self and achieve their former performance levels following SCI. This can, and occasionally does happen. However, as Frank (1995) makes clear, problems arise when people become fixated on one type of body, and sense of self, in circumstances where the restitution narrative is not appropriate. As the words of Matthew, Mark, Eamonn, and Richard indicate, under such circumstances individuals find it hard to remind themselves that other body-self narratives might have to be found, experienced, and told. However, without an increase in their narrative resources and a willingness to contemplate options with regard to constructing alternative identities, the space and opportunity for these men to craft who they want to be, and can be, would appear to remain constrained and limited for the time being. Quite simply, when it comes to restorying the body-self, people cannot transcend their narrative resources.

It would appear that Matthew, Mark, Eamonn, and Richard have yet to find ways, or are unwilling, to connect their own experiences to those of others to form a 'collective story' (Richardson 1990). This kind of story, deviates from mainstream cultural plots and legitimates a replotting of one's life by emotionally binding people together who have had similar experiences. This binding has the potential to overcome the isolation and alienation felt by many because it links separate individuals into a shared consciousness so that social action is possible. In the absence of such a collective story, the possibilities for social action and change are limited. The adherence of these men to a reliance strategy is also limiting because, as Gerschick and Miller (1995, 203) have indicated: "men who rely on dominant conceptions of masculinity are much more likely to internalize their feelings of inadequacy and seek to compensate or overcompensate for them." Since the problem is perceived to be located within oneself, rather than within the social and political structure, this model does not deconstruct, interrupt, or challenge, but rather perpetuates the current gender order and associated able-bodied regimes. As a consequence, the experience of Matthew, Mark, Richard, and Eamonn as men with disabilities gained through sport highlight, what Gerschick and Miller (1995) see as the insidious power and limitations of contemporary masculinity. Finally, their emotional stoicism along with the narratives that have been made available in the past, and are available now to these men through the world of sport, are extremely problematic in terms of enabling them to construct different body-self relationships in the future.

Notes

[1] We would like to thank the English Rugby Football Union, and their Sports Injuries Administrator, for allowing us to gain access to players who have experienced SCI through playing this sport. However, the views expressed in this chapter are entirely our own and should not be taken to represent those of the English Rugby Football Union, or their Sports Injuries Administrator.

[2] Following Charmaz (1994), social identities derive from community memberships and cultural meanings that others confer upon them. Personal identity, outlines a sense of differentiation, continuity, location, and direction by and in relation to self. These identities then become part of a self story, which is both relatively coherent and supple enough to undergo transformation. Additionally, athletic identities become tangible documents which, for example, reconstruct part of the physiology and surface of a body. Consequently, athletic identities become physical or embodied parts of a self story

References

Brock, S. C & Kleiber, D. A. (1994) Narrative in medicine: The stories of elite college athlete's career-ending injuries. *Qualitative Health Research*, 4(4), 411-430.

Brewer, B., Van Raalte, J. & Linder, D. (1993) Athletic identity: Hercules' muscles or Achilles' heel? *International Journal of Sport Psychology*, 24, 237-254.

Bury, M. R. (1982) Chronic illness as biographical disruption. *Sociology of Health and Illness*, 4(2), 167-182.

Bury, M. R. (1991) The sociology of chronic illness: A review of research prospects. *Sociology of Health and Illness*, 13(4), 451-468.

Charmaz, K. (1987) Struggling for a self: Identity levels of the chronically ill. In: J. Roth & P. Conrad (Eds), *Research in the Sociology of Health Care: A Research Manual, Vol. 6*. Greenwich, Connecticut, JAI Press Inc.

Charmaz, K. (1994) Identity Dilemmas of Chronically Ill Men. *The Sociological Quarterly*, 35(2), 269-288.

Connell, R. (1995) *Masculinities*. Cambridge, Polity Press.

Csikszentmihalyi, M. (1993) *The Evolving Self*. New York: Harper Collins.

Curry, T. (1993) A little pain never hurt anyone: Athletic career socialization and the normalization of sports injury. *Symbolic Interaction*, 16(3), 273-290.

Denzin, N. (1989a) *Interpretive Biography*. Sage, London.

Denzin, N. (1989b) *Interpretive Interactionism*. Sage, London.

Frank, A. (1995) *The Wounded Storyteller: Body Illness and Ethics*. Chicago: The University of Chicago.

Frank, A. (1998) From dysappearance to hyperappearance: Sliding boundaries of illness and bodies. In: H. J. Stam (Ed), *The Body and Psychology*. London: Sage.

Gadow, S. (1982) Body and self: A dialectic. In: V. Kestenbaum (Ed), *The Humanity of the ill: Phenomenological Perspectives*. Knoxville, TN: University of Tennessee Press.

Gerschick, T. J. & Miller, A. S. (1995) Coming to terms: Masculinity and physical disability: In: D. Sabo & D. Gordon (Eds), *Men's Health and Illness*. London: Sage.

Harris, I. (1995) *Messages Men Hear*. London: Taylor & Francis.

Hickey, C., Fitzclarence, L. & Matthews, R. (Eds), (1998) *Where The Boys Are*. Deakin: Deakin University Press.

Kleiber, D., Brock, S., Lee Y., Dattilo, J., & Caldwell, L. (1995) The relevance of leisure in an illness experience: Realities of Spinal Cord injury. *Journal of Leisure Research*, 27(3), 283-299.

Leder, D. (1990) *The Absent Body*. Chicago: University of Chicago Press.

Mathieson, C. & Stam, H. (1995) Renegotiating identity: Cancer narratives. *Sociology of Health and Illness*, 17, 283-306.

Maykut, P. & Morehouse, R. (1994) *Beginning Qualitative Research*. London: Falmer Press.

Messner, M. (1992) *Power at Play: Sport and the Problem of Masculinity*. Boston: Beacon Press.

Messner, M. (1997) *Politics of Masculinities: Men in Movements*. London:Sage.

Messner, M. & Sabo, D. (Eds), (1990) *Sport, Men, and the Gender Order*. Champaign, IL: Human Kinetics.

Murphy, R. (1990) *The Body Silent*. New York: Henry Holt.

Nauright, J. & Chandler, T. (Eds), (1996) *Making Men: Rugby and Masculine Identity*. Cassell: London.

Richardson, L. (1990) *Writing Strategies*. London: Sage.

Seymour, W. (1998) *Remaking the Body*. London: Routledge.

Shakespeare, T., Gilespie-Sells, K. & Davies, D. (1996) *The Sexual Politics of Disability*. London: Cassell.

Sparkes, A. C. (1996) The fatal flaw: A narrative of the fragile body-self. *Qualitative Inquiry*, 2(4), 463-494.

Sparkes, A. C. (1998) Athletic identity: An Achilles' heel to the survival of self. *Qualitative Health Research*, 8(5), 644-664.

Thornton, A. (1993) The accomplishment of masculinities. In: T. Haddad (Ed) *Men and Masculinities*. Toronto: Canadian Scholars Press.

Toombs, K. (1992) The body in multiple sclerosis: A patients perspective. In: D. Leder (Ed), *The Body in Medical Thought and Practice*. Dordrecht: Kluwer Academic.

Wolcott, H. F. (1994) *Transforming Qualitative Data*. London: Sage.

Wolcott, H. F. (1995) *The Art of Fieldwork*. London: Sage.

Martti Silvennoinen

ANGUISH OF THE BODY

This tale has been maturing slowly, over the course of a few years, among my many autobiographical tales. All my stories about childhood have had a more or less obvious shared warp thread: the experiential body of a boy. As a rule, my own memories have been linked with sporting experiences: being giddy with excitement, accomplishing daring feats, feeling joy, but also with the other side of corporeality: shame and fear.

What unites the rapidly shifting emotional states of the story is a transformation where the harmless body becomes a troublesome one, the focus of one's whole awareness. As a text worked up for publication, 'Anguish of the Body' may seem to amount to intimate voyeurism. But is this an accurate judgment after all? We have all our familiar everyday bodily experiences that have been made public by being told to other people, as well as those tabooed ones that took place 'behind the curtains' – but that are all the same familiar and shared.

December 1996

It is a Monday evening in early December. I am sitting alone in the living room watching the Seven O'Clock News. Sampo, my six-year son and his friend from the floor below who is a year younger, are busy in Sampo and his big brother's room. Sampo has asked me to go to the storeroom to fetch a doll and a push-chair. I'm taken aback. What's the idea, two boys playing mummies and daddies?

The boys wanted to build their make-believe home in a confined square bounded by a bunk bed, a desk and two walls. To get in you had to climb into the top bed and drop down. I though the idea dubious until I realised that it was just what I would myself have constructed as a little boy; a small and exciting lair.

The news are sparkling into my eyes and a torrent of words is filling my half-sleepy being as I hear running feet and Sampo's shrill cry: Daddy, my willy is bleeding!

He rushes before me, with the friend close at his heels. It is true! Drops of blood are gushing down to the floor. In my thoroughly alarmed state I am hit by the idea that something horrendous has happened; simultaneously, for an instant, there flashes before my eyes an image where it is myself who is standing there on the floor. A shared moment of fear!

At lightning speed, I drag the boy to the toilet and tell him to stand over the toilet bowl. I dash to the kitchen. As I tear the ice cubes from the fridge freezer out of their mould into my hand, I find that they are shaking like possessed. Utterly forgetting the hot-water trick I simply smash the mould against the sink edge. Finally I manage to grip an unbroken ice cube into my hand, pressing it against the tip of the willy. A shout of pain! The friend is standing mute at the door.

When the blood starts to congeal I carefully pull the foreskin back. Goodness bloody gracious! There is a deep pulpy wound under the glans. What on earth has happened?

Discreetly, I begin to question the boy and promise him a visit to the health centre as soon as there is a little less bleeding. Sampo's initial shock is beginning to abate and he tells, sobbing, that in the daytime he had fallen down in the courtyard of the day nursery and a small stone might have got into his pants then. I point out that in that case bleeding would have begun immediately, not only now. And a stone could not have penetrated his winter clothes.

When I have stuffed into the boy's pants a diaper of toilet paper, we go out and walk to the car. During the drive, Sampo never stops asking questions. What will they do to me at the health centre? Will they prick me? Must I stay there? Will they put me to sleep (an obvious memory from a few years' back when Sampo's torn tongue had to be stitched)?

I soothe the boy and begin to weave the plot of the story. Playing mummies and daddies?

When Sampo ran into the living room, his willy was still erect. Accordingly, the boys had compared their penises or just shown them to each other. As a symbol of daddyhood? The taboos of my own childhood pour into my mind. What would my mother have said in a similar situation: See how God punishes you! Let this be a lesson for the future!

At the health centre, when the nurse behind the reception desk asks about the reason for our arrival, Sampo turns so visibly pale that we are led to a consulting room where the boy can lie down.

It is a tight spot. You must pick your words with care. How to take up what I think happened? There on the bed lies an anxious boy, worried about the fate of his projection and undoubtedly also about the shame of being found out.

I say that I want to speak with him before the doctor comes to examine him. I tell a story of my own about playing mummies and daddies, drawing on my own experiences. Sampo may fill the tale in. Yes – willies had been shown around – and somehow, when the boys had been entering or was it leaving their nook of a home (with pants down), Sampo's willy had got caught between the side of the bed and his own body. A wound! Apparently caused by a thumbnail?

The doctor comes in, asks questions and examines Sampo. I say a few words about the plotline and Sampo, too, manages to make his contribution. The doctor takes a look at the willy and then looks the boy in the eye: It's home for you. It will be as good as before – then turns to me and adds: Sprinkle it with warm water two times a day. That's all. When we drive home we are already laughing over the matter.

Nevertheless, for a few days the willy becomes a 'centre of life'. Every time when it bleeds a little when it is washed with water, Sampo bursts into tears. It'll never get well! Pissing is full of drama. Will there be blood? The first thing the boy does in the morning is to take a peep at the paper diaper in his pants. When the day finally arrives when there is no blood and no hurting, you can actually see how the small body lets go.

October 1947

I remember the white washroom of the Kuopio County Hospital. I am crying inconsolably and clinging to my mother. I do not want to stay there. The washer lures me to take a shower. Just for a little moment. I go. But when I step back from behind the shower curtain, my mother has left. I realise that the grown-ups have succeeded in their plot. I have been betrayed. Abandoned!

I lie on the narrow table of the operating room, strapped down. I gaze at the high windows across the room. I have been told that my hernia will be operated and that they will put me to sleep. Suddenly someone behind me covers my face with an etheriser cap. The windows begin to whirl round. I feel that I am suffocating. I am unable to cry out or free myself. Is this death?

Next morning I am being sick into the washbasin of the toilet. I have taken a secret drink of water despite being very strictly forbidden to do any such thing. The stitches might open! Being put to sleep with ether makes you feel sick. I am told that with an empty stomach makes it a little better.

The boy standing before the washbasin next to mine is scrubbing the stumps of his fingers with a small stiff brush resembling the kind you use for washing clothes. His operation wounds have healed but I suppose brushing keeps bugs away. A home-made gun has blasted away four fingers from his other hand. There is just the thumb jutting out. I feel sorry for the boy.

As far as I can remember I stay at the hospital some two weeks and make friends with the 'fingerless'. He is the only one there who chats to me, at the same time relieving my longing for father and mother. During all that time my parents are not allowed to visit me in the children's ward. There is the danger of infection.

The day comes when the stitches are taken out with little pincers. They pinch a little, but a healed-up wound is a sign that I have got well and shall be allowed to return home; to my games with my friends. A foreign lump the size of an egg has been removed from the right side of my lower abdomen. There is a scar of some ten centimetres. It will be there until the end. As a memory of my body.

EXTREMITIES

David Brown

THE SOCIAL MEANING OF MUSCLE

This chapter traces embodied experiences of becoming, and being a competitive male bodybuilder within the subculture of British bodybuilding. Creating a hyper-muscular male body presents a prime example of what Shilling (1993) has referred to as a self-reflexive body project. This work draws on life history narratives to inform how the male body 'under construction', provides tangible evidence of self-transformation, leading to reconstructions of identity. The sensual embodied nature of these body projects highlights that the development of a hyper-muscular body is neither a disengaged symbolic act, nor an act of docility (Foucault 1977), but lived in a phenomenological sense. These men's bodies communicate identity through their presence, form and what they symbolise (Goffman 1969). With increasingly successful investment of the body and self into this project, muscle, and the lifestyle engaged in to construct it, become imbued with changing meanings.

The social and cultural identity of bodybuilder is reflexively configured (Giddens 1991): The continuous modification of narratives of the self is required in order to accommodate physique developments and responses to them, both personal and other. Self-reflexive body projects of competitive bodybuilders are also fraught with dilemma and contradiction. As Sparkes (1996) notes, self-empowerment through investment into a body project is existentially fragile; the threat of bodily injury, illness or failure severely damages the ability of the individual to maintain self identity through the bodybuilding project. However, as the bodies and the stories told about them become reconstructed over time, a sense of existential control over the creation and definition of self (Wacquant 1994), in which living to achieve something and be some-body, become strong narrative themes giving personalised meanings to muscle and the lifestyle engaged in to construct it. Through these stories, there is a strong sense of empowerment and emancipation from former selves brought about by the bodybuilding project.

The Study and Participants

The study used a life history approach as the primary method of data collection. Along with this a participant observation of gym life was also used to help establish a context of the participants in their gym settings. The life history interviews, conducted over twelve months, attempt to offer insights into key moments of these men's lives in 'intertextual' and 'intercontextual' ways so that the "stories can be 'located,' seen as the social constructions the are, fully impregnated by their location within power structures and social milieu" (Goodson 1995, 97). Whilst much of this chapter is presented as a realist tale, I nevertheless attempt to resist 'taken-for-grantedness' of realist writing that Sparkes (1995, 165) warns is a "'safe' but ultimately 'disembodied', neutral voice, a universal human subject outside of history who is hermetically sealed off from social categories".

Following Richardson (1992) and Sparkes' (1994) calls for researcher reflexivity, my position as a white, mesomorphic, working class male, with a personal history of bodybuilding style training, implicates me as author, given the life story that I inevitably bring to the process of collecting, interpreting and representing other's stories in life history contexts. However, I am not a bodybuilder, although for a short period of my life I would have described myself as such.

The five participants considered here were sampled following Glaser and Strauss' (1967) processual description of these, four are competitive bodybuilders, Jeff, Joe, Paul and Mike. The fifth, Frank is a strength athlete. The principle characters of focus are the first four. Introductory descriptions given here refer to the present as the period when data were collected. Although Frank's narrative enjoys limited exposure it provides an insider account of bodybuilding culture and dispositions.

Joe is twenty-three, he was born just outside London, is currently engaged and lives in the South West where he moved to in his mid teens. He already has nearly eight years training experience, has competed at National level twice as a junior, placing in the top five in each and now manages a gym. Following an extended period of injuries, Joe is now back in training for a his entry into the senior categories. Joe is nevertheless an advanced bodybuilder. Jeff is thirty-one, divorced and remarried with children. He is a self employed finance salesman, currently in training for his first show after approximately seven years of bodybuilding; he is an advanced bodybuilder.

Mike is thirty, divorced, a builder with three years of bodybuilding training behind him. He is preparing for his first show, next year, and will compete as a first timer in the novice class. Mike has rapidly progressed to an advanced level of development. Paul, is thirty, unmarried, works as a hospital porter and doorman and is the most advanced bodybuilder here, he has been training for approximately eight years and has placed well in two senior British finals, one in the top five. Paul is currently training for more body mass so he can compete at a larger size. He aims to win the Britain's and qualify for the amateur Mr Universe. Frank, is in his early thirties, he does not describe himself as a bodybuilder but as a strength athlete. Frank's main interest is in training for performing lifts, he is currently in training for a car lift for cancer research.

The Beginnings of a Body Project

All of the participants were stimulated to start bodybuilding in earnest (as opposed to more recreational forms of weight training) when they first visited a bodybuilding gym. They were stimulated by the visual display of male muscle in these gyms. Acts of embodied communication assume a special significance in space restricted gyms or bodybuilding shows, where the body and its display are social statements. The participants here all associated with the images they saw and responded to the hyper-muscular physiques on view when they first entered the gym as beginner weight trainers, Joe recalls:

> Yeah, you know, I looked at him and I thought, you know (...) he's huge, he's massive he's huge (...) there's what I wanna be like really (...) It's something like that where you can walk into a place and you can dominate, well not dominate but maybe impress just solely through the way you look (...) um and you know it sort of brought his character across, because you had to take notice of him (...) I suppose it was one of the things I was always looking for but you don't realise until you actually see somebody who is like that.

Both Mike and Paul had been training in small non-commercial rural gyms before moving to bodybuilding gyms. Mike recalls his first night there, "Yeah, I remember the first time us ever went up there, from Ideford, our little gym like, up there it was just (...) huge." Mike was (in context) referring to the male bodybuilders' physiques not the gym itself. Paul's reaction was similar: "So of course we went to the Power-house in Saintsville, saw all these big guys walking around and I think that's where things started bells ringing. Yeah, I saw this guy walking around there, fourteen stones, I thought he was a monster." The term monster in bodybuilding is for males, at least, a compliment on their development, Paul's continues:

> Yeah (...) when we went up to have a look at the gym, When I started looking at these guys I looked and they looked like warriors, they were just fucking awesome (...) yeah.

These men displayed what Goffman (1963, 33) describes as a shared understanding of shared 'body idiom', "bodily appearance, and personal acts, dress, bearing, movement, and position, sound level, physical gestures (...) and broad emotional expression." Fussell's (1991) description of 'the walk' – where his newly acquired bodybuilding friends taught him how to walk 'like a bodybuilder' – although romanticised, is a fine example of body idiom. Joe's comments capture this idiom when he expressed his opinion that, "the body speaks for itself". Similarly, when Jeff said that, "'the way people see me and perceive me without saying words is nearly as accurate as they could describe me as a person", he was pointing out his view that his body carries the person he wishes to present.

Giving precedence to form over function, bodybuilding places value on the visual image (Dutton 1995) and a form of hedonistic aestheticism is projected in the image for the viewer – who can also be the self via a mirror. The bodybuilding idiom centres on a competitive *anatomical elitism:* a hyper-developed body, on display, erect in posture, lifting heavy weights, lean, defined and pumped. All the participants reported deriving pleasure and interest from observing their own and other male physiques in this way. Frank summarised this succinctly:

> You can actually not like someone but actually like their physique, you're not actually gay or anything like that but you can appreciate you know the work put in looks good, it's good.

What is regarded as anatomically elite has symbolic masculine connotations, as Paul's description of top professional bodybuilder, Paul Dillet, illustrates:

> Yeah he's going to be something to be reckoned with (...) you know he's the perfect triangle man (...) wide shoulders, massive shoulders, tiny little waist, big back, massive legs and calves (...) very symmetrical, very athletic like the (...) Greek Gods you know. That's what it's all about.

The sensual, embodied, display of 'male power' at shows and in the gym stimulated the participant's fascination. Jeff summarised his involvement as, "I have always appreciated anything to do with power (...) basically things that are powerful, I like the look of a person with a good physique." For Jeff the image of power is symbolically fused with that of the hyper-muscular male body. The 'look' of power is significant, Paul concurred with Jeff and remarked that bodybuilding for him was an 'extension' of his fascination with power. The hyper-muscular male physique is alive with imagery for Paul; as notions of Greek god's and warriors suggest, Paul's vision of the bodybuilder included size and shape. In deciding to pursue the development of an anatomically elite body themselves, these men have all, in their own ways invested themselves into a project of the body, a project which through its iconography is instilled with hegemonic masculine ideology see Connell 1995), where hardness, physicality and control are combined with exaggerated Greek aesthetics and given value.

In addition to the visual allure bodybuilding training offers something more organic. Sensuality that comes with training, feeling the muscles work, pump and grow were part of the fundamental attraction to train with weights. All of the participants enjoyed hard training from the outset. The elusive 'pump' – the rush of blood into a working muscle – is a powerful experience that left them wanting more and still does, as Mike describes: "I think once you've done it, it's enjoyment, it's just feeling (...) you cannot describe it (...) the blood is just full on, that's how it should be." Joe and Paul talk of similar experiences:

> If I have a day where I use a lighter weight and the movement stills feels good where I feel the same sort of adrenaline then it doesn't really matter, it's basically how the muscle feels. The term loosely is pumped. If it feels pumped, full and its been worked then that makes you feel good and that's basically what I'm striving for.

> On a good day a good workout it's wonderful, a little bit stronger, a massive pump, and your energy levels are still high, the whole zest of it all. You walk out of the gym really good, tired but really good.

Frank also recalls similar experiences of the pump during a particularly memorable workout:

> It's about an hour and a half's drive form here to Trymquay at the time, and a tremendous depression all the way there, right I get into the gym, and um walk through the door, do the warm up still not feeling like training, and all of a sudden change, immediately. Started training extremely, you know heavily, I'm getting everything out, walking out the gym and just like I've been on LSD or something, which I've never taken but you know a really good high feeling. Everything's gone all the endorphins have kicked in.

A combination of the visual and the physical stimulated desire in the participants, Joe was soon making new commitments: "The effort was being made in the gym to do it and the question in my mind was how big can I get?" Paul pointed out that his first trip to a bodybuilding gym was "where things started bells ringing."

Transforming the Body.
The Bodybuilding Lifestyle

When Jeff, Mike, Joe and Paul moved to the gyms described above and began training harder, and more frequently, their lives began to change. Paul remembers this period:

> Well, it started trickling in I'd say the interest. The gym was crap that I was in. Course, that's when I moved away and decided I liked the feel of the muscle pump. Well, this is it you know, just look good, feel good. It's good while you're just building yourself up, then you start getting into the nutrition side of things. I packed in smoking, I was only smoking one a night but it was enough really. It's a whole lifestyle.

Joe welcomed the changes:

> I felt more comfortable with myself after lifting weights (...) The attitude was very positive when I lift weights, I felt a better person (...) and um you know (...) From there to where I am now it's become a hobby, it's become more of a lifestyle and it's just developed.

A key feature of the bodybuilding lifestyle is that it is 'anthropometric'. This involves the regular measurement and monitoring of body size, composition, performance, recovery, ingestion and excretion. Jeff's comments here show clearly how the these monitoring techniques effect his life:

> My food, has to be structured towards a high carbohydrate, high protein, every two and a half to three hours intake, diet. My rest has got to be considerably more than somebody who has a much easier time. So I sleep in the afternoon and have a nap normally two hours in the afternoon. On top of that I sleep at least eight hours every

night, sometimes nine. So, uh and on top of that I have to make money! And on top of that I go out once a week and have a few beers to (...) um live like a normal person. Apart from that, that's about it.

Jeff did not mention that his training consisted of between four and five sessions per week in more than one gym, one of which was almost a one hundred mile round trip. Mike's attitude is similar because he also travels to train and is spending all available money including tax money to buy good food and steroids, so that by next year he can enter competition at the highest possible level. Whilst these lifestyles might seem excessive they are not unfamiliar stories as Klein (1993) and Fussell's (1991) experiences already indicate. Field notes also showed this to be common with other bodybuilders in the gyms studied. Indeed Paul has come to view his successful physical transformation as the result of his strict disciplined lifestyle:

I mean there're guys that go in the gym and give it their all, there's guy's like me who (...) that go in their all and plus, and then you add everything else into it; dieting side of it I mean you've got these boys who are eating the same amount of food as when they first started (...) and wonder why their growth peters out. But then they put it down to steroids: 'Oh, you wouldn't get that big without steroids,' and I say: 'Here's some steroids, see you try to get this big.' Because they can't because they're not eating enough, they're not putting enough into it, their outside life doesn't correspond with gym life and it throws the two apart. What you do outside the gym is big difference to what happens inside. You've got to eat proper food and nutrition, sleep, get it right and take it to the gym. It's only thirty per cent gym work goes to making up physique; the rest of it's food and nutrition.

Foucault's (1977) interest in the disciplined body was how the state maintained power through the individual. These bodybuilders are exemplars of the how networks of power enter the lives of individuals, although closer attention to these body projects shows discipline via self-monitoring and techniques of the body being used for purposes other than the production of socially 'docile' bodies. This is an irony that Foucault, in his later work (1980), became aware of. A 'conscience of self-knowledge' exhibited in the self monitoring anthropometric lifestyles of these bodybuilders is not as socially and politically docile as it may theoretically seem.

Lifestyle regulation here is in pursuit of something that is far from close to 'normative' life, conduct and appearance. Moreover, drug taking, severe dieting and intense training are potentially health threatening (see Klein 1995), and in the case of chemical enhancements is now a criminal activity. Therefore, as Foucault (1980, 56) reminds us, "suddenly what made power strong becomes used to attack it." Paul has become implicitly aware of this situation: "It's gone a bit further than for health, you've made your body stronger, puts lot of strain on your body joints and that you're asking a lot from your heart." Mike agree's with Paul:

So I say this is bit more than keep fit (...) and then they think that cos you do all the bodybuilding that you're a keep fit fanatic, which you're not really, it's not really healthy lifestyle.

Over an extended period the four bodybuilders here have achieved startling physical transformations through increasingly disciplined lifestyle practice and hard training. All of these men regard the initial years as a period of muscle *accumulation*. Joe's current disposition is typical:

To compete at that level (seniors) you have to take time out to be able to progress. Really it's unlike any other sport, it's not like playing tennis or squash or even snooker or pool it's something that takes time to build and develop.

Joe's outlook dovetails with Bourdieu's (1990) conception of 'physical capital'. The investment of the physical and emotional self, time and economic resources is as Shilling (1993) points out an exercise fraught with risk when the site of investment is the body. Nevertheless, as their bodies transform, the symbolic value associated with them changes, and with it possibilities for conversion into other forms of capital such as cultural, social, economic and even 'existential' capital. Existential capital refers to the ameliorated sense of self-identity and purpose relation to the self and others through the bodybuilding project.

An example of this is when Paul became Mr ***** Coast, his physique had been given a new meaning, a status. By converting physical capital into cultural capital – he had arrived as a successful national standard bodybuilder. He also gained economic capital through the sponsorship he attracted allowing him to prepare better for the British Finals. In another way Paul successfully converted his physical capital into social and economic capital when he became a regular and sought after doorman around the town. Similarly, Joe only began defining himself as a bodybuilder after he had successfully won his first show and qualified for the British finals:

> Bodybuilding is at its penultimate (...) is to be on stage and competing (...) you can really turn round to somebody and say that you are a bodybuilder when you've been on stage and competed and you've done well and you get recognition from that.

Joe's knowledge and appearance have also seen him successfully convert physical into economic capital as the former gym owner, who helped him prepare for competitions, subsequently offered a job as gym manager, a post he still holds.

New Body. New Identity

Through the successful accumulation of muscle, these men have converted, muscle into social, cultural, and economic capital. These changes hold symbolic value for their sense of self as a form of existential capital. Viewed in this way, we see a picture of the social meaning of muscle emerging and its direct relationship with the developing body and enhanced self and social identity.

Notions of becoming and being a bodybuilder are author imposed, overlapping categories. There is no objective measurement or definition of what constitutes being a bodybuilder, much of this is a matter of personal opinion. Nevertheless within the culture of bodybuilding itself there are criteria; a combination of muscular size, condition, training intensity and success in competitions. To fulfil one or more of these four general criteria will bring *recognition*. Given Turner (1984, Bourdieu (1993) and Shilling's (1993) contention that there is a constant society wide power struggle over what constitutes the legitimate body and legitimate uses of the body. The transition from 'Other' to bodybuilder for these men, lay in recognition that is the outcome of a reflexive engagement between the individual's body-self and person's bodybuilding peers and social interaction more generally. Frank's point illustrates this:

> Some places are very hard to break into. You either have to be training there for very long time to actually get in, and gradually you get to know someone or you've got to go in and do something special; then your in straight away. I say straight away, they don't always accept you straight away, they recognise you.

All the participants were aware of responses to their changing states of physical development. However bodybuilders appear to draw definite distinctions between the value of comments by respected bodybuilding peers and those made by 'lay' people, not adequately experienced to judge the bodybuilding physique. Jeff pointed out that the content of normal people's responses to his development didn't matter because his standards "were higher than what they're seeing." "What they see and what I see are to different things." Paul, Mike and Joe agreed on this, again Jeff's comment was typical: "People used to say core you're looking good mate, you're getting bigger," and I'd say "'yeah, thanks very much, you know, but it wouldn't go no further than that."

Synnott's (1992, 102) thesis that "society, mind and body are all linked in ways that are still being discovered" is strongly reflected by the participant's stories. The medium for this linkage would seem, in part at least, to be the social significance of identity. Goffman's (1969) dual conception of identity helps clarify the reflexive process. Social (virtual) and self (actual), identity are interlinked and the individual has to adapt feedback on one's social identity in order to maintain a stable sense of self identity and vice versa. Through their life history narratives these bodybuilders pinpoint significant moments of change and in so doing revealed something of the processes by which these occurred.

The social construction of identity, has, for these men, been a reflexive or two way process involving their changing bodies and others' changing reactions to that transformation. Jeff admits, "sometimes I don't realise how big I am." Similarly Mike has had some difficulty coming to terms with his own view of himself with that of how others now see his physique. In particular he realises that it's " 'hose people who haven't seen you for a long time" who notice change the most. Paul's social identity as a bodybuilder has been constant for a number of years now but he can still remember a key moment that altered his perception of himself:

> When I was going to shows and seeing my mates, in these shows, the Wessex and the NABBA and so on I remember seeing these big guys walking around, not competing, the guys that never compete but they're always massive I always used to be saying to my mate, "look at the size of him over there look". And then it came to the stage where I can remember walking out of the seating area of the show at the end of the night, well it might have been the prejudging and there was a load of young chaps there and they go look at the size of him, I overheard them as I walked (laughs) by and I was with my girlfriend and my mate I heard them saying this 'over there' something like that, and it suddenly dawns on you.

Now, by contrast, he admits that the responses from those outside of bodybuilding 'can get on your nerves,' he recalls:

> When I was working on the doors and that (...) you always get comments (...) you know you get too much coming in (...) people always asking you: Oh, is that all you under that suit or cor you've got bigger tits than my missus (...) It's always at you so it's nice to get away from it.

By contrast, the cultural identity of bodybuilder is far more discerning and whilst confirmation with normal people generally revolves around size, peers cast a far more discerning gaze and judge with a critical eye, as Joe point's out:

> It's nicer to be big, I'd sooner be the weight I am now rather than what I was six years ago. Basically it's a gradual progression, but with progression a lot of big guys are without the quality of muscle so my personal opinion is not only being bigger than the average

person, but having better quality muscle rather than just a 'blob', you know a big physique.

When bodybuilders refer to someone as 'big', this implicitly refers to large, lean, shapely muscle. Mike recognised the importance of peer approval following a chance meeting:

> You never think you're big enough like, till you go out and think Christ, and other blokes tell you, big blokes. Last time I got a load of (steroids) (...) A couple of others said (...) Christ how much are you now? I know I hadn't been up there for six/eight months, I went up there and went to an all night club, course I went in there and they could see then, so I've grown over a period of time.

Mike's delight at other bodybuilders and most importantly 'big blokes' acknowledging his progress is highly significant for his sense of self. Other trainers in the gym also give important feedback in terms of progress and reaffirm the cultural status enhancements that come with muscular size and shape, as Mike indicates:

> But tis a good rush I think. Yes, yeah, cos like years ago, I'd look a somebody and think look at the size of him. When you're at that stage people come up to you and say (...) And they come to you.

> You look down at people – looking at me training (...) They're training for what I look like now (...) Nothing else compares to it really, it gives you the edge yeah, you know gives you more confidence.

Paul concurs:

> Cos you forget you know you take all this (his size) for granted, I take all this for granted and yet as soon as you walk into a foreign gym, you get the same response all over again. It kind of makes you feel like a bit of a celeb! It's quite funny.

Mike, Paul, Jeff and Joe's investments in their body projects, although not finished, have generally been successful. The reflexive nature of the bodybuilding project requires significant others for confirmation of a bodybuilding identity. To have a culturally accepted bodybuilding identity, positive peer review is essential; positive review converts physical capital into social, cultural and symbolic capital. In view of Giddens' (1991) self-reflexive projects, constant adjustments are being made to maintain a stable sense of self. In Goffman's (1969) terms this requires balancing self identity with perceptions of social identity. Moreover the degree to which these bodybuilders are aware of and happy with their investments is not be underestimated as Mike and Jeff point out:

> Yeah bodybuilding because you see it's what you wear with you 24 hours a day, whereas any other sport, it doesn't. But that doesn't mean to say you do it because that's what you want everyone to see (...) You do it for yourself, because it makes you feel good.

> Yeah, but actually it's the only sport that you carry around with you 24 hours a day, you know. Something like golf, stick your clubs in the boot, you come home, put them away.

A Self-Creating Body Project

> "I live my Body (...) The body is what I immediately am (...) I am my body to the extent that I am." (Sartre 1966, 34)

One of the ironies of corporeality is that although our bodies are unfinished at birth we cannot ever *totally* finish them. Our bodies will inevitably breakdown and die at a point before we could ever make a reasonable claim that we have finished our work on them or achieved their inherent potential. Considering Shilling's (1993, 175) view that "irrespective of modern technological advances, death remains a biological inevitability that is ultimately outside human control," it may seem more than a little strange that people like Paul, Mike, Joe and Jeff should bother to invest so much of their lives into constructing a body. However, that they willingly spend their lives on such a project tells us something about the human condition and body-self relationships, that might transcend male bodybuilding.

Following Beck (1992) and Giddens' (1990) theses, an individual's self identity is constructed in a reflexive modernity characterised by existential uncertainty. The social significance of the lived body in attempting to creating a stable sense of self is an important, if, problematic recognition (see Shilling 1993; Shilling & Mellor 1996). Jeff's comments illuminate his disposition:

> Yeah, put it this way, I look at it this way. I'm always going to be young, within myself, no matter how old I get (...) right? Now, bodybuilding can't stop the body from decaying as you get older, but, it can certainly slow down the process, and with that (...) I've also got a very positive mental attitude, all the time while you're bodybuilding, because it's not something you can take lightly.

Given this context, the dominant, competitive masculine dispositions in evidence in these men's body projects, suggest Wacquant's (1994) description of the 'irony of masculinity'. The need to be the antithesis of femininity is an unobtainable identity because it has no definite location. Yet this ever present *dynamic tension* drives these individuals to ever greater creative *and* destructive limits. The hegemonic masculine drive towards achievement, elitism and winning in bodybuilding requires being anatomically as big as possible; as in Mike's view, "You're trying to get as big as you can, I'm unfit as buggery really." Developing the body is an unending task; Jeff acknowledges and embraces this saying, "the day I'm the size that I want to be then I'll stop, right. But I hope that day will never come." Of course that day will never come because as Mike realises, "But its some (...) Just an aura really, you think...you never think your big enough, Anybody you talk to thinks (...) never big enough."

However there is an existential turn (see Warnock 1971): One of the strongest suggestions of this study has been the relationship between these participants' sense of self and their body projects in the context of their perceptions of what it means to live a worthwhile life. The culmination of these forms of physical capital converted into a socially symbolic achievement, a radical, masculine, statement of self in society, Paul captures this mood succinctly:

> I'm only five eight at eighteen stones (...) far more impressive, a lot of people like I was saying earlier on, people like me at sixteen stones, but I like to be, you know, big, freaky big and very blocky, wide.

This is an existentialist body project par excellence in that the individual engages in self defining, self creating acts. The body takes a central role because as Shilling (1993, 184) points out "the ability to construct a reliable self-identity through the adoption of lifestyles, which have at their centre a concern with body regimes is inextricably concerned with control." In the face of ontologically challenging or fateful moments the existential nature of their bodybuilding narratives demonstrates an ambivalence towards the prospects of death, ill health and injury. Indeed the perceived *duty*, is to live to achieve something and *be* somebody. Paul and Mike's most recent injuries left then unable to train their legs. Their reactions are typical:

> The last time was cor fucking hell the pain, that's the biggest thing it's god I can't train, god I can't train. I always think its good when you reach that stage, you know when you got to do it.

> I should have, come the next workout when I had legs, stayed with the same weight and not gone up, but again there's this feeling in the back of your head, go for it (...) size, strength (...) muscle, and it overrides that, and course two or three weeks after that it's a problem.

Mike's response to the notion of ill health and death from his lifestyle is equally typical, "at least I'll look big." The prospect of dying fat prompted Joe to point out, "I don't want to go out like that, not even in death." Joe and Paul's comments show a similar disposition, concerning steroids, the lifestyle and its dangers:

> Um but that side doesn't worry me too much, I know the risks what are involved, I know what can happen, my ideas towards it have changed an awful lot since my mum died, she died very young, uh she had cancer. Basically she didn't drink she didn't smoke, she didn't drive fast, she didn't get any real buzz out of anything (...) she sat down she watched T.V. and she died of cancer. So the way I look at life is make the most of it while you can. Um as far as that issue is concerned with the use of the drugs side of it, if at some point I feel that I want to take them, I feel I've only got one life and however short it is (...) if it's something I feel I wanna do then I will do it (...)

My idealism has changed, life's too short to restrict yourself on (...) If you want to do something, saying no because other peoples' fears and principles have influenced you in the past not to do it, you know.

It's gone a little bit further than for health, you've made your body stronger, puts a lot of strain on your body joints and that, you're asking a lot from your heart (...) you know (...) it's better than smoking twenty fags a day (...) yeah the way you look; the way you feel about yourself; if you feel good, feel strong; keeps you young; it definitely keeps you active. That's the only thing, you know, blokes my age now, married, pot bellied and couch potatoes. You've got to work at it, it keeps you young.

Considering Heidegger's (1927) conception of Angst and Giddens' (1991) questioning of ontological insecurity felt in high modernity, ascribed social identities move to the level of the personal with the individual left to 'create' an individuated identity. Reflexivity both helps and hinders control of the body and identities derived from it. As Beck (1992, 135) points out, the process of individualisation changes how we see the world so that, "the temporal horizons of perception narrow more and more, until finally in the limiting case history shrinks to the (eternal) present and everything revolves around the axis of one's personal ego and personal life." Jeff implies this directly:

I think the thing about that is that it's not a reality (...) it's not reality (...) if I had this if I had that you know if I if I if I (...) if I if I if I is very derogatory in my book. What I got, that's what matters.

Concluding Comments

Mike, Paul, Jeff and Joe's hyper-muscular bodies have, over a period, come to act as existential mediators for a sense of self identity. In other words the body, lived in the present, provides links between past and future selves. Whilst undoubtedly imbued with hegemonic masculine associations, the reflexive nature of the bodybuilding project, the body and sense of self created, has led to their embracing a philosophically existential disposition that attempts to address ontological uncertainty or Angst. The social meaning of muscle for these men represents a withdrawal to their bodies construct an individuated identity. Control of the body remains a practice that individuals in high modernity can attempt to create some meaning. It would be folly to ignore the potential for self-empowerment (of both sexes) offered by the ascetic and aesthetic dimensions of developing a hyper-muscular body.

The pursuit of a bodybuilding project has provided these people with a lifestyle that *they perceive* offers them the potential to make a radical statement of their masculine selves. Additionally the body-building project is self perpetuating, embodied experience for these people. The sensuality of pain and pleasure are very real; training for the pump, lifting heavy weights, seeing and feeling the body transform in growth and contest preparation phases offer a way of living that stimulates on a daily basis.

All the participants considered that the dangerous practices they engaged in were risks worth taking, when compared to the act of living one's life to the fullest possible achievement of a self enhancing goal. The pleasure and satisfaction they drew from this are testimony to these existential values lived through he body. Concerns over health and longevity are disregarded as less important than 'achieving' and 'living' a materially enhanced existence in the eternal present where that materialism is of course the hyper-muscular body. Being and having a body remains a paradox of the self, for these bodybuilders being means having, and having means being.

References

Beck, U. (1992) *Risk society*. London: Sage Publications.
Bourdieu, P. (1990) *The logic of practice*. Cambridge: Polity Press.
Bourdieu, P. (1993) *Sociology in question*. Lodon: Sage Publications.
Connell, R.W. (1995) *Masculinities*. Cambridge: Polity Press.
Dutton, K. (1995) *The perfectible body: The western ideal of physical development*. London: Cassell.
Fussell, S. (1991) *Muscle; Confessions of an unlikely bodybuilder*. New York: Scribners.
Glaser, B. & Strauss, A. (1967) *The discovery of grounded theory*. Chicago, Ill: Aldine.
Giddens, A. (1990) *The consequences of modernity*. Cambridge: Polity Press.
Giddens, A. (1991) *Modernity and self identity*. Cambridge: Polity Press.

Goffman, E. (1963) *Behaviour in public places*. New York: The Free Press of Glencoe.

Goffman, E. (1969) *The presentation of the self in everyday life*. Harmondsworth: Penguin Press.

Goodson, I. (1995) The story so far: personal knowledge and the political. In: J.A. Wisnieski & R. Hatch (Eds) *Life history and narratives*. London: The Falmer Press.

Heidegger, M. (1963 [1927]) *Being and time*. Oxford: Blackwell.

Klein, A.M. (1993) *Little big men: Bodybuilding subculture and gender construction*. New York: State University of New York Press.

Klein, A.M. (1995) Life's too short to die small: Steroid use among male bodybuilders. In: D. Sabo, & D. Gordon (Eds.) *Men's health & illness*. London: Sage, 105-120.

Foucault, M. (1977) *Discipline and punish: The birth of the prison*. London: Allen Lane.

Foucault, M. (1980) Body / Power. In: C. Gordon (Ed.) *Michel Foucault power/ knowledge*. Brighton: Harvester, 55-62.

Richardson, L. (1992) The consequences of poetic representation: Writing the other, rewriting the self. In: C. Ellis & M. Flaherty (Eds.) *Investigating subjectivity*. London: Sage, 125-137.

Sartre, J-P. (1966[1943]) *Being and nothingness*. New York: Washington Square Press.

Shilling, C. (1993) *The body and social theory*. London: Sage.

Shilling, C. & Mellor, P. (1996) Embodiment, structuration theory and modernity: mind/body dualism and the repression of sensuality. *Body and Society*. 2 (1), 1-15.

Sparkes, A. C. (1994) Life histories and the issue of voice: Reflections on an emerging relationship, *International Journal of Qualitative Studies in Education* 7, 165-183.

Sparkes, A. C. (1995) Writing people: Reflections on the dual crises of representation and legitimation in qualitative enquiry, *Quest* 47, 158-195.

Sparkes, A.C. (1996) Interrupted body projects and the self in teaching: exploring an absent presence. *International Studies in Sociology of Education* 6 (2), 167-187.

Synnott, A. (1992) Tomb, temple, machine and self.: The social construction of the body, *British Journal of Sociology*, 43 (1), 79-110

Turner, B. S, (1984) *The body and society*. Oxford: Basil Blackwell.

Wacquant, L. (1994) Why men desire muscles. *Body & Society* 1 (1), 163-179.

Warnock, M. (1971) *The Philosophy of Sartre*. London: Hutchinson University Library.

David Jackson

WARRIOR SPORT.
GRAMMAR SCHOOL RUGBY
1956-1959

As in a fog, I heard the platform voices
hectoring and braying, "Forget the pain!"
"Forget the pain!"

Like in a slow-motion film, I unscrewed
my head from my hacked at limbs.
I turned my hurting body into a concrete block.

Through the wreathing mist the enemy came.
Their forward rush smashed through our defences.
I curled my body around the flying ball
clung on, clung on, a cradling stockade
in a whirl of boots.

Their studs ground deeply into my muddied buttocks.
Their cries and curses were all around me.

Inside the school assembly walls,
underneath the fake, hammerbeam roof
I saw the team and Headmaster applauding.

Under the stuffed, caribou head,
beyond the golden Scroll of Honour panel,
the ghosts of Suez were lurking.

As in a dream, I saw Captain Oates
dissolve into the shrieking blizzard
without looking back at his little tent.

And Captain Nevill, the first day of the Somme,
kicking a football into No Man's Land.
Cut down while dribbling towards enemy.

So I don't caress my stinging buttocks with pride.
I don't want to be mentioned in dispatches
and then dumped.

I holler out in outraged pain.
I laugh aloud at the crumbling
sons of empire.

The ghosts begin to fade.

Mikko Innanen

SECRET LIFE IN
THE CULTURE OF THINNESS

A Man's Story

Opening

The text is based on a diary that I kept for about a year, beginning in July 1996. I had just separated from my common-law wife and gone to a kibbutz in Israel to escape a life that had become intolerable. During our relationship, which lasted some two years I lost a normal relationship with food at the age of 24. The diary, which I named "Reality Bites", represented an attempt to understand the links between this break in my own identity, the interruption of my body project, and our broken relationship. The text is about how the physical body is bound up with the illusory but pragmatically necessary coherence of a 'self' and with human relationships; it connects an observation about body projects (Shilling 1993) with the self-reflexive process that according to Anthony Giddens (1991) is a central feature of Western civilisation. These two projects come together in stories and narratives that we constantly reproduce in new versions (Sparkes 1996).

25 July 1996
I do not want you to come here to Israel just for my sake. I have

been thinking and I realised that I want you here partly because it would give me a chance to enjoy things. You have taught me that fat and calories are sinful, that filling your stomach is in fact something negative. That's why we had all those innumerable unspoken rules. All that I eat here in Israel feels somehow sinful. If you saw me next time ten kilos heavier I would feel that I have not followed your instructions.

I don't think that I am like I once was. Some of the things that I experienced with you have changed me. I would like to become as I used to be and I have this feeling that I need your permission to do so.

You suggested a sweet strike, that we would not eat after six in the evening. You began to buy carrots, cabbages and things like that to avoid calories. You even gave up alcohol completely because of those calories. And I have followed you step by step. I thought that maybe I would be able to "get out" if you would show me that it was all rubbish and lies. You asked me to step into a leaky boat, rowed it in the middle of the lake and now you want to leave me there alone. Maybe you are right and each of us must get away from there on his or her own, maybe to opposite shores.

My Illusion

Two years before my journey to Israel I began to be irresistibly attracted by this beautiful woman – and particularly by her figure – four years my junior. I felt that I was head over heels in love. Conquering her became as if an obsession because every time I felt that I had got close she suddenly disappeared from my side without being able to explain the reason. I was baffled.

She was a former competing athlete and any outsider would have thought that she has not the least reason to be dissatisfied with her body. At the time I imagined – took it for granted – that voluptuous women like her would bear their curves with pride and happiness. After a brief courtship she moved to my flat. Soon I noticed that something was not right. She herself found her body, which I adored, problematic. She was beset with deep feelings of dissatisfaction and uncertainty and a profound sense of inferiority because of her figure. She told me that for a few years now she had been suffering from compulsive eating disorder and asked me to help her in her attempts to make her life easier.

28 July 1996

My head is like a Ferris wheel. Sometimes I blame you for what happened, sometimes I reproach myself. Two days ago we agreed on the phone to break up. I had so hoped that you would come here to Israel for a week. That hope was not fulfilled. I wanted to show you here – far from the imprisoning framework of memories – that I am ready to admit my mistakes and accept you as you are. My weakness must have made your problems worse, at least their external manifestation has changed shape. You no longer eat compulsively and your body is now completely without fat.

I do not know why, but even before I began to go with you I knew that it would not last forever. I told my thoughts to a friend, but I still wanted to get on your train. It soon became clear that the gap between our hopes, goals and abilities is too huge. All the same, neither of us was strong enough to change the way things were. Maybe that was why we picked up food as the third wheel in our relationship, to structure our life and to link us. It created a sick, dangerous dependency between us. We both hate it but at the same time it was what we needed. Why the hell didn't we have the wit to end our harrowing life together sooner? Why did we keep banging our heads together even when there was no promise of the shared future that I longed for?

I am a fragile weak shit. What is called empathy or commitment can in my case also be called timidity, inability and a complete lack of courage. I suspect that that's my real mirror image. That may be why I wish that the skin stretched around me would adjust itself to the prevailing norms of collective acceptance.

That was how I saw myself immediately after the break-up. I had no understanding whatever of what food dependency is all about. I thought that those who suffer from compulsive eating disorder must control their food intake and eat in moderation. My idea of a remedy was essentially wrong. Our life became – at least from my point of view – a shared project whose focus was her eating, body and balance of mind.

The control that I went in for and that she asked for was on the one hand hateful to her, on the other hand she wanted me to maintain it. We exercised like mad and ate smaller and smaller amounts of more and more "healthy" food. Control and rules were followed by her lapses, the deep self-pity that they caused and by an even more severe ascesis. I was very ill equipped to cope with this conflict and with the "breakdowns" of my partner that went with it.

The best thing about our relationship, a passionate sex life, began to dry up. We were too tired and I too committed to monitoring her body to be able to enjoy the joys of love. I had got myself caught in the most ambivalent situation. I became dependent on the control that I was maintaining. I could not stop even though I understood that things were going badly wrong. At the same time I began to grow estranged from my own body. It was as if a dissatisfaction with my own body that had lain dormant somewhere within me had come to the surface. I became conscious of the flesh enveloping my bones. I was completely unable to accept myself as I was. I grew estranged from my own body and simultaneously from other people.

I now think that I saw in this communal slimming a chance to supplement a personal "body project" that I had started while still a child and that had gained impetus in my student years. My mother built the family life of my childhood around food, and food had in my family a very important symbolic function linked with maintaining an experience of communal life. I was a roly-poly little boy whom the other boys living in our little locality sometimes teased. Nor was my position improved by the fact that my father was a clergyman. I was a clumsy clergyman's son. As a result, I have been dissatisfied with my body as long as I am able to remember. I knew from experience that I lacked the willpower to keep up the kind of diet and training regime that I assumed would be required to achieve a dream body. I hoped to finally succeed by linking my own project to hers.

In a way I did succeed. When our relationship began, neither of us was overweight from the point of view of health science. Nevertheless, during the two years that we spent together we lost a total of 30 kilos. My earlier "harmless" diets certainly gained new impetus. Finally we were both very thin – but ever more dissatisfied with ourselves and with our bodies – tired and baffled. The promised salvation never arrived. We felt weak and wounded. As for a life outside our relationship, practically speaking neither of us had any. And our own relationship, it was as worn-out as its riders.

After my flight to the kibbutz my own misery only increased. My slimming got completely out of hand. I regulated my eating more strictly than ever. I thought about food all the time and found other people's company distasteful. I was living alone with my body. I ate just enough to be barely able to manage my daily assignments on the kibbutz. However, in my free time I additionally lifted weights and took 1.5-kilometre swims in the kibbutz swimming pool. I had jogged before, but now it became simply too hard. Every bite of food must be legitimised by expending it immediately.

In the evenings I often found myself drifting hungrily around the kibbutz kitchen. One evening I found in a cold store the remains of the snack served earlier that evening. We had been given sausage rolls. What was left was mostly puff pastry that looked delicious after having been fried, and I piled a big heap into a plastic bag. I intended to eat this tasty find in a controlled manner. However, after the first bite I lost command and gobbled down the whole heap of pastry. The self-control that I had developed over years broke down for the first time. I went to the weigh-lifting room with my stomach full of puff pastry. I lay on my back on the wrestling mat, exercised my stomach muscles and wept. At that moment I understood what her illness was all about. I had myself caught the same disease.

Corporeal Identity

The body and corporeality have become one of the central objects of research in social science. This revival of interest in the body has led us to a clearer conception of the complexity of the relations between the body and the self (Sparkes 1996, 463). According to Mike Featherstone (1991), consumer society has joined forces with the body's self-preservation instinct, which encourages the individual to adopt instrumental strategies in the battle against decay and deterioration. Machine has become a frequent metaphor for the body, the term body maintenance being a good example. Our relationship with our body begins to follow the same orientation, guided by instrumental rationality, as our relationship with consumer goods. Work for the aesthetic body is rewarded by an experience of spiritual salvation or even by improved health, but such work is also linked with the way we present ourselves in public and with the generation of a self possessing a higher market value. The desirable and desiring body has been pronounced a means of pleasure: the closer a body is to the ideals of youth, health, fitness and beauty, the higher is the market value of the self and, simultaneously, of the body. (Featherstone 1991, 170-171, 177) Women (and today also many men) are, naturally, aware that the main motive of slimming is cosmetic and that "looking good" is not only a precondition of social acceptance but that it may also be a key to a more exciting lifestyle. The body is our pass to all the good things of life. (Featherstone 1991, 182, 185, 186)

According to Andrew Sparkes (1996), the physical body is completely bound up with the self and with human relationships. He argues that body projects (Shilling 1993) and the self-reflective process (Giddens 1991) combine in stories and narratives that we produce in constantly new versions. In postmodern society an individual is assumed to adopt, at different times, distinct identities that do not come together around a coherent self. These identities can be contradictory and point to different directions, with the result that the subject is in a state of constant change (Sparkes 1996). If we perceive ourselves as possessing a unified identity spanning all of the period between our birth and death, it is because we have constructed a personally pleasing narrative of ourselves, a "self-narrative" (Hall 1992, 275-277). If a coherent self is, as is argued by postmodernists, an illusion actively generated and maintained by humans, it is also an illusion necessary for our perception that we are living a controllable life in a knowable world. When a person interacts with themselves and with other people, the importance of this illusion is, paradoxically enough, very real (Sparkes 1997, 86).

The idea of identity as an illusion does not conflict with biographical studies, in my opinion quite the contrary. Donald Polkinghorne (1995, 5) defines narrative as text, as discourse, organised by plot. A plot makes the events of a life intelligible. By focusing on how identity is constructed and how it changes over time, for example, biographical research may be able to offer important perspectives on how a self-narrative is constructed and how it is constantly changing in relation to the surrounding cultural system (Hatch & Wisniewski 1995, 123). The strength of the biographical approach lies in its ability to concentrate on stories that tell us about an individual self and about personal experiences. (Sparkes 1997, 105). This involves interpreting narrative texts that have been written in specific situations and from specific positions (eg Sparkes 1995; 1997).

7 November 1996

The fact that because of your compulsive eating I was never really clear about what would happen next made me invest all my resources into maximising the predictability of the future. Maybe control of eating came about because of it, too. Today I recalled an evening in July 1995. You were going to a housewarming party given by a friend of yours. I had learned to fear situations where you found yourself without me before tables groaning with food because they could trigger off an attack of binge eating. I was in great distress and hoped that you would not leave. I remember how I wept and asked you to hold my hand and say that you understood my fear. You, however, went away and left me on the couch weeping the tears of the misunderstood.

I drank and wrote poems in which I told that I could not cope with the situation. I left the poems on the windowsill and went out on the town. I felt as if I had been run over by a street roller. I was sitting on the terrace of a restaurant when you came, strangely enough in a sympathetic mood, to fetch me away. I was drunk, but not all that much. At home you were as distant as when I had left and went to bed. I lay down beside you. I wept and shivered, wanting more than ever before to be held in a lap and understood. You slept. I remember how I tried to dig myself into the space between the wall and the bed. I felt as if my head was going to burst from pain. I got no understanding whatever. I felt as if I had been mentally raped. I went to another room to sleep on the floor. I waited for you to come and comfort me. In vain.

In the morning I finally came back to lie down beside you. I still felt like crying, while you threatened to leave me. We were supposed to be going to a rock festival with a friend of yours and you said that you would go without me. I would be left languishing on my bed. In such a state of mind, when I implored you not to leave me, I felt that I was abandoning my own self. The Mikko who knew that he had a right to be weak and a right to be understood and loved and a right to occasionally need support and encouragement, departed. He was replaced by a person who adjusted himself to the situation. That adjustment meant denying one's own needs and body. They were replaced by coldness, lack of emotion, concentration on external things, finally by becoming a total outsider to one's own life. A kind of mental death. An year after that evening I was at a very low ebb. Weak and without self-respect. I was so anguished that I wanted it to be seen also in my physical appearance. I was not permitted to enjoy things, to be psychically weak or physically strong.

Interpretations

I find it difficult to pinpoint the moments in this autobiographical study when data-gathering came to an end and interpretation began. It is impossible to define the boundary between the personal and the interpretive text with any degree of precision. In my diary I was trying to find a way to make my identity continuous. How had another person or illness become a part of me and what was it that had caused it? On the other hand, what was it that had turned me into another person?

For a long time I was totally clueless. I kept blaming my partner for what had happened, unable to admit that I had myself become ill. As I was searching for my lost self I stumbled on the five-stage model of "dramatic self-change" outlined by Athens (1995). The model is a logistic one, but for me reading it was a release. That was precisely how my life has been running! First the individual, going through a fragmentation stage, is forced to witness a splintering primarily of their own self. In the provisionality stage the individual is desperately struggling to put together a new unified self to replace the old one that has fallen to pieces. In the praxis stage the individual must conjure up the courage and confidence to trust to the reunited self by trying it out in practice. When the new unified self has withstood this test, the individual must, in the consolidation stage, patiently wait for the desired social feedback on their new achievement to generate the psychological power required to internalise the new unified self. Finally, during the social segregation stage, the individual must, without exception, strive towards those groups where they feel most at home and draw away from those groups where expressing the new self is most difficult. Thus, according to Athens, once begun the process of dramatic self-change can never come to a completion.

In our attempts to make our self cohere we come face to face with the multiplicity of identities and body projects that are linked with the course of our life. For Sparkes (1997, 102) this raised the question of how we manage to take the changes in our self into account in a way that enables us to reflect the social that is surrounding us while simultaneously still maintaining at least some minimum continuity of self. Another question that interested Sparkes concerns the ways in which people revise their self-narrative when they are trying to make sense of changes in their self and identity. This question is particularly interesting in cases where a body project has been interrupted and given up for good, with the result that the self that we thought we were and that we attempted to maintain no longer resolves into anything that would be intelligible in its new context. (Sparkes 1997, 102)

I had reached adulthood when I lost a normal relationship with food and with my own body. And I who had been thinking that eating disorders are the kind of problems that beset adolescent girls! A person falling ill with an eating disorder is forced, apart from living through their interrupted body project, also to reflect on the psychic starting points of their illness. The situation is particularly difficult when the patient is an adult male. It has been argued that when men fall ill, it is often the first time when they come to realise that the physical body is bound up with the masculine self and with human relationships (Young, White & McTeer 1994, 186-187). According to Kathy Charmaz (1994, 269-279), illness affects mens' masculine self, normally taken for granted, raising questions of identity that may come up again and again. When a man's ability to perform in some of the areas where manhood is proven is weakened, he loses characteristics that he values, physical functioning capabilities, social roles or personal goals, and his masculine identity is often undermined.

Consumer society demands that we keep our body under control, but the pathogenesis of anorexia or compulsive eating disorder is also affected by the patient's relations with his or her significant others; with family and other close relations and friends. Despite leading to a state of physical weakness, anorexia is primarily a psychic condition.

According to Conrad (1987), disease may be seen as an undesired physiological process or state. Illness may further be described as a social and psychological phenomenon linked with these assumed physiological problems. Thus illness is a thoroughly social phenomenon that may or may not be grounded on disease as a physiological finding. Illness is more a matter of consciousness, behaviour and personal experience than of a physiological process. (Conrad 1987, 2) I have aspired towards past identities. However, the realisation that identity work is always directed towards the future has gradually freed me to break myself away from the past.

According to Martti Silvennoinen (1999), the culture of science and scholarship is sometimes too heavily built on the fear of losing face, and on the devaluation of everything that is personal. It doggedly shirks from greater reflective sensitiveness and from "emancipatory regression", nor does it encourage the members of the scientific community to recognise differentiated and polyphonic "small worlds". An autobiographical approach, one's own life and one's own writing activities are bound up with experiences and consciousness. At the same time it is a question of authenticity, with the qualification, however, that here good answers are neither positive nor negative. It is impossible to recall original experiences, even bodily ones, as such. A writer must accept that the life transferred through writing onto a "verbal stage" may be a matter of hidden narratives and fixations (Vainikkala 1998). Nevertheless, I still think that the strength of the biographical approach lies in an ability to focus on stories that tell us about people and their lived experiences.

Epilogue

An earlier version of this paper was presented at a conference in the USA in autumn 1998. That version ended with the Interpretations chapter. This time, however, I wanted to write a concluding section where I reflect on my attitude to research of this kind and give the woman of the story a chance to speak for herself.

Questions of intimacy are important in research. They are particularly important when we are writing about others. Even when we are writing about ourselves we often cannot but write also about other people. The purpose of this text, too, was to describe my personal feelings rather than dissect other people's character. Nevertheless, in order to write about myself I had to also write about the other party of our relationship. Accordingly, I wanted to have also her permission to publish the text. We met and I gave it her to read. She granted her permission for its publication, answering with the following feedback.

Reality Bites, but Rewards in the End –
The Woman's Side of the Story and Reply to That of the Man's.
Oh dear, oh dear, isn't it so, that everything that doesn't kill you makes you stronger? In a way I am happy to have experienced something like that; I would hate to be a person who has not seen the dark side of themselves and who has not experienced something as drastic as the whole episode was.

I am just so glad it is all over. The problem is still there, but in a far more tolerable form and I am concentrating on other things. I am sure my thesis would be done by now had I paid as much attention to my studies as I did to different kinds of nutrition books and calorie tables!

Accepting yourself the way you are; that's so difficult. The pressure from outside does not make it any easier. According to the media one should be beautiful/handsome, successful in one's work, popular (especially among the opposite sex) still kind, gentle and empathetic. I think the problem with myself was the difficulty of expressing negative feelings. It is not until have reached the age of 20 that I have allowed myself to be tired and weak, scared and disappointed and not always so nice to everybody. It is not until now that I've grown to know myself better, including the scale of my negative feelings. And that has made me, I hope, a both more tolerant and tolerable person.

In addition to presenting the view of the "Other" I also want to reflect on my attitude towards research of this kind. Before I began this paper I could not understand how a chap like me, intelligent, well-educated and reasonably successful, could be caught in a situation where one is positive that one is no good, unsuccessful and disgusting. Writing this paper and reading, as a part of the writing process, narratives discussing corporeality and identity and their link with close human relationships, have given me an opportunity to understand the events of my past.

I have also, in my work as a researcher, interviewed other men who have lived in similar relationships. I have noticed that nice and responsible men – the kind of men among which I somehow include also myself – who find the central meaning of their life in human relationships are liable to adopt their partner's troubles as their own. In such cases, the impact of communication at cross purposes, when the loved one says that she cares for you but simultaneously indicates her rejection, may be crushing. My own experiences no longer feel at all extraordinary and my relationship with food and my body has also become considerably more relaxed. Life is once more "ordinary". Nevertheless, I often find myself thinking about the personal and professional risks involved in writing of this kind. Do I really want You as a reader to know about these things? What are you thinking about my work? What are you thinking about me?

I have given my text to a few people to read, and all experiences have not been particularly encouraging. After reading the text some have marvelled: is that how you really are? Are you so crumbly? I do not recognise myself in such descriptions. All the same, I decided to take the risk and publish my text. I know that I have something to say. A central factor in this decision was a talk with an interviewee who has lived in a similar relationship. Someone living with a person suffering from an eating disorder easily find themselves very alone. Alone – and bewildered. Accordingly, he thought that it was of primary importance that eating disorders should be discussed in public, particularly while also paying attention to the position of the other party of any marriage or live-in relationship involved in the situation.

Acknowledgements

My thanks to Martti Silvennoinen and Arto Tiihonen for their critical and supportive comments on an earlier draft of this paper. A special thanks to Andrew C. Sparkes for helping me to understand the embodied nature of identity. Big thanks to Hannu Hiilos for translating the text.

References

Athens, L. (1995) Dramatic self-change. *Sociological Quarterly* 35 (3): 521-532.

Charmaz, K. (1994) Identity dilemmas of chronically ill men. *Sociological Quarterly* 35 (2): 269-288.

Conrad, P. (1987) The experience of illness: Recent and new directions. In: J. Roth & P. Conrad (Eds.) *Research in the sociology of health care: A research manual* (vol. 6, pp. 1-31). Greenwich, CT: JAI.

Featherstone, M. (1991) The body in consumer culture. In: M. Featherstone, M. Hepworth & B.S. Turner (Eds.) *The body.* London: Sage, pp. 170-196.

Giddens, A. (1991) *Modernity and self-identity.* Cambridge: Polity.

Hall, S. (1992) The question of cultural identity. In: S. Hall, D. Held & T. McGrew (Eds.) *Modernity and its futures.* Cambridge: Polity, pp. 374-425.

Hatch, J. & Wisniewski, R. (1995) Life history and narrative: Questions, issues and exemplary works. In: J. Hatch & R. Wisniewski (Eds.) *Life history & narrative.* Lewes: Falmer Press, pp. 113-135.

Polkinghorne, D. (1995) Narrative configuration in qualitative analysis. In: J. Hatch & R. Wisniewski (Eds.) *Life history & narrative.* Lewes: Falmer Press, pp. 5-23.

Shilling, C. (1993) *The body and social theory.* London: Sage.

Silvennoinen, M. (1999) Unpublished manuscript.

Sparkes, A. C. (1995) Writing people: Reflections on the dual crises of *representation* and legitimation in qualitative inquiry. *Quest* 47, 158-195.

Sparkes, A. C. (1996) The fatal flaw: A narrative of the fragile body-self. *Qualitative Inquiry* 2 (4): 463-494.

Sparkes, A. C. (1997) Reflections on the socially constructed physical self. In: K. Fox (Ed.) *The physical self: From motivation to well-being.* Champaign, IL: Human Kinetics, pp. 83-110.

Vainikkala, E. (1998) Minä, lukijani, kaltaiseni [I, my readers, people like me]! In: K. Eskola (Ed.) *Elämysten jäljillä. Taide ja kirjallisuus suomalaisten oma-elämäkerroissa* [In search of personal experiences. Art and literature in Finnish autobiographies]. Helsinki: Suomalaisen kirjallisuuden seura, pp. 437-467.

Young, K., White, P. & McTeer, W. (1994) Body talk: Male athletes reflect on sport, injury, and pain. *Sociology of Sport Journal* 11, 175-194.

METAMORPHOSES

Douglas A. Kleiber & Susan L. Hutchinson

HEROIC MASCULINITY IN THE RECOVERY FROM SPINAL CORD INJURY

Introduction

> Traditional assumptions of male identity, including an active, problem solving stance, emphasis on personal power and autonomy, and bravery in the face of danger form a two-edged sword for men in chronic illness. On the one hand, these assumptions encourage men to take risks, to be active, and to try to recover which certainly can prompt recreating a valued life after serious episodes of illness and therefore, bolster self-esteem. On the other hand, these assumptions narrow the range of credible male behaviors for those who subscribe to them. (Charmaz 1994, 283)

What began for us as a fairly straight-forward analysis of themes of activity participation following spinal cord injury has become a deeper reflection on what it means for a man to 'recover' from a spinal cord injury (SCI). This chapter describes the basis for our conclusion that vigorous physical activity (and particularly sport involvement) is at best a temporary palliative to 'the crisis' of physical disability for spinal cord injured men and at worst an impediment to a more complete personal transformation following the injury experience.

In this chapter we take the crisis of physical disability for men to be a crisis of de-masculinization (Gerschick & Miller 1995; Sparkes & Smith 1999; White et al. 1995). Some of what it means to be a man in western culture[1] – as reflected in bodily performance, sexuality, power and strength – is threatened by the loss of physical function that accompanies spinal cord injury. On the other hand, transcending the limitations imposed by SCI, however it might be accomplished, not only promises to mitigate the most visible source of threat to a man's identity – a failed body – it also bestows on him an even more dramatic masculinity, that of the archetypical *hero*.

It is ironic that Christopher Reeve, an American actor who personified the idealized hero in his portrayal of the American superhero *Superman*, is now the most publicly visible spokesperson for people with SCI, having been so injured himself (Maddox 1996). His message that "we ought not think anything is impossible" perpetuates societal beliefs that heroic effort, even in the face of overwhelming odds, is *the* best response to SCI, and the best expression of that attitude is in the resumption of aggressive physical activity. While an emphasis on traditional masculine achievement and expression is cultivated in physical rehabilitation contexts throughout the world, especially in the elite wheelchair sport movement, we suggest that such emphases following SCI make healthy recovery and adjustment for men more difficult in some respects. By promoting aggressive, risky, physical self-expression and celebrating physical prowess, and in defining recovery as a *heroic* process, rehabilitation establishments circumscribe recovery in ways that limit the possibilities men see for transcending their injuries and using the experience as an opportunity for personal growth.

We focus here on men for two reasons: 1) we take as our problem, with the other authors of this volume, the ways in which embodied experiences are particularly important to expressions of masculinity; and 2) we recognize that men, as a result of gendered patterns of action, are far more likely than women to incur a spinal cord injury (National Spinal Cord Injury Statistical Center, USA 1996). While we also recognize that much of the post-modern thinking about masculinity recognizes its multiple, unstable, contextual, problematic, contested and often contradictory constructions (cf. Cornwall & Lindisfarne 1994; Kimmel 1987; Kimmel & Messner 1993; Mac an Ghaill 1996), this chapter will not argue for re-interpretations of maleness, manhood or masculinity, nor will we review recent literature that addresses these issues. Rather we will focus on the ways that traditional masculine ideals impact men's adjustment to spinal cord injury. We draw on the metaphor of the hero to argue that traditional masculinities are at least as much a constraint as a resource in the adjustment process for men with spinal cord injury.

The previous chapters in this volume speak in some way to both the individual athletic experience and its significance in personal development and transformation. This chapter departs from that pattern in two respects. First, while we will continue the use of narrative analysis, we will examine the experience of a *group* of people, namely individuals who have experienced a spinal cord injury. Second, and more importantly, we will examine sport not as the problematic terrain of the athlete, but rather as an attractive – but nonetheless problematic – solution for the person for whom previously-available athletic alternatives have either been substantially reduced or eliminated or were never there in the first place.[2]

We turn first to laying out a theoretical framework for answering the question of how vigorous physical activity is both a solution to the crisis of physical disability following spinal cord injury and a problem for subsequent adjustment and development. We then consider the ways in which *depiction* of heroic action in rehabilitation and in wheelchair sports provides a *narrative map* (Pollner & Stein 1996) that charts a course for doing what needs to be done to be a 'good man' after spinal cord injury. To elaborate our critique we draw on vignettes of men who have acquired spinal cord injuries that have been published in disability magazines. Our interpretation of these stories is that they tend to perpetuate an idealized prototype of a 'good' rehabilitation story, one centered on a hero metaphor. In these magazines the life stories of men who have acquired spinal cord injuries are reconstructed primarily in terms of aggressive action and heroic transcendence of physical limitations. The 'culturally elaborated' nature of bodies and selves intersect in these portrayals with personal interpretations of what it means to be both disabled *and* a hero in the struggle and triumph experienced by these men.

Masculinities and the Hero Metaphor

Our Western culture loves heroes. We want to make those men and women who face extreme adversity our heroes; we admire them for their bravery and courage, and we want them as models for our own forms of struggle and citizenship. But with men this traditional hero form is particularly problematic. Where 'masculine' is constructed around a 'compulsive warrior' mentality (Robinson 1995) it locks men in to a singular and inherently limiting pattern of masculine behavior.[3] To be a man in our culture, according to Robinson (1995, 137-138) means being "tough, physical, athletic, fearless, powerful, competitive, aggressive, superior, ruthless, logical, shrewd, conquering, financially successful, unemotional, uncomplaining, and correct." While Robinson is describing a reckoning that takes place for many men at midlife, his ideas are consistent with the struggle to survive adversity at any point in the life course.

> This model also teaches men to override their needs and limitations and learn instead to. (...) push onward relentlessly in spite of fatigue, hardship, illness, or desire (...) 'When the going gets tough, the tough get going' and ' no pain, no gain' are slogans of this masculine ideal. Breaking down, giving up, being needy, being sad are all reasons for shame in this model. We believe there is no beauty in failure.

The loss of stereotypically masculine characteristics that accompany the loss of bodily function (independence, sexual potency and strength) is the source of the crisis of physical disability for most men. Regaining some or all of these characteristics becomes part of a heroic quest for triumphant recovery. In fact, the hero metaphor as a narrative genre predominates autobiographical accounts of illness survivors who present their stories as battles to be fought and won (Frank 1995; Hawkins 1993).

Hawkins (1993) suggests that sports and hero metaphors are re-plete with images of enemies and allies that are implicit in competitive discourses of victory over one's body or illness. In the disability maga-zines we examined this was clearly evidenced; in one story we are told that a former motocross champion "did rehab the way he did moto-cross – 110 percent. And he battled anger and denial with the same perverse dedication" (Vogel 1995, 22). Such a pattern is striking in the degree to which it mirrors the culture's traditional visions of masculinity. Strong, competitive, driven, and unemotional, successful spinal cord injured male patients are often portrayed as fighting – and winning – the battle over their broken bodies. As such, they embody the traditional hero in Western culture. The hero metaphor provides a man an alternative image of being – when he is no long able to walk.

Heroic Masculinities Following Spinal Cord Injury

Spinal cord injury impacts nearly every aspect of daily life, from the additional time needed to dress, travel and eat to dealing with architectural and attitudinal barriers that dramatically affect a disabled man's view of himself and his world (Kinney & Coyle 1989). In addition to facing physical and social challenges, disability presents 'identity dilemmas' for men. Problems of forced passivity, becoming dependent or subordinate threaten taken-for-granted masculine identities and lead to identity dilemmas that make men's adjustment to disability difficult. (Charmaz 1994, 280). Charmaz pointed out that disability becomes even more defining when "men draw upon the existing cultural logic that currently defines masculinity as they try to make sense of their altered selves and situations." Many of the men with chronic illnesses that Charmaz interviewed exerted considerable effort to preserve their images of what it meant to look like a normal man. Holding on to these masculine ideals gave some of the men in her study the hope that they would be able to recapture their past selves.

Kewman and Tate (1998, 150) suggested that a man whose 'premorbid personality style' is one of strong attachment to traditional masculine identification is particularly vulnerable to depression and maladjustment following spinal cord injury. The losses associated with SCI for these men lead to "feelings of decreased physical and sexual prowess, promoting lower self-esteem, loss of male identity, and feelings of guilt and overall loss of control." This loss of self was evidenced in the narrative accounts of young men who became quadriplegics as a result of rugby injuries (Sparkes & Smith 1999). For these men, the differences between who they had been as highly regarded rugby players, and who they saw themselves as quadriplegics were irreconcilable.

Through interviews with men with disabilities Gerschick and Miller (1995) interpreted the dilemma of being a man and being disabled as a tension in which a man finds himself at the intersection of two conflicting ideologies, that of hegemonic masculinity which demands strength, and the stigmatization of being disabled, which implies weakness. They found that men responded in two different but not mutually exclusive ways to this tension: reliance on dominant concepts of masculinity, by emphasizing control, independence, strength, and concern for appearances; or rejection of dominant constructions of masculinity and disability. They concluded that adjustment to disability was more difficult for men who relied on dominant conceptions of masculinities:

> [These men] are much more likely to internalize their feelings of inadequacy and seek to compensate or overcompensate for them. Because the problem is perceived to be located within oneself, rather within the social structure, this model does not challenge, but rather perpetuates, the current gender order. (Gerschick & Miller 1995, 203)

Feminist researcher Susan Wendell (1989, 116), herself disabled, suggested that heroic efforts by individuals with disabilities to fit within our able-bodied society have led to the creation of even greater divisions between this world and the majority of people who are disabled and who do not or cannot live up to this heroic ideal. In particular, she is critical of the honor that is bestowed on people with disabilities for "performing feats of physical strength and endurance."

These perspectives, coming from fields as diverse as sociology, men's studies, and disability studies, share a common critique of the place of traditional masculinities in the lives of men whose sense of self is threatened by illness or disability. For some, embracing traditional conceptions of masculinity may be a source of strength and hope. But for the majority of men with disabilities, the 'otherness' suggested in the hero model may further distance them from both personal and social integration, and ultimately, from personal growth.

Portraits of Heroic Masculinity Following Spinal Cord Injury

We did not initially come to the data with a critical perspective; instead we shared an assumption that leisure or sport has a positive influence on adjustment. In many ways we saw leisure – in this case, primarily wheelchair sports participation – as a solution to the crisis of physical disability for men with SCI. Over forty biographical vignettes, presented in three disability magazines were first examined for evidence of continuity and discontinuity in recreational, sport and leisure pursuits following spinal cord injury. While we did find some evidence bearing on our original questions, a more dominant theme emerged, particularly in the men's stories – a theme consistent with what we have since called the hero metaphor. The consistent, almost stereotypical, treatment of the men in these reports drew us to analyze these vignettes from a critical perspective.

Sources of Data

A systematic document analysis was subsequently undertaken with all editions of *Spinal Column* magazine published between 1994 and 1997. *Spinal Column* is the primary publication of a major rehabilitation facility in the Southeastern United States. Two other magazines were selected to compare and confirm the findings from our primary analysis of *Spinal Column*: the 'Special Images' section of a rehabilitation products catalog, and stories and letters to the editors in *New Mobility*, a magazine which highlights technology and athletic achievement. Only those covers or stories pertaining to men with spinal cord injures were included in this analysis. Of the 16 editions of Spinal Column magazine published over the four year period studied, 11 featured as their cover story men who had acquired a spinal injury. Two of the other five editions also featured men: a man who had acquired a brain injury and former United States Presidential Aide, James Brady, who was visiting the rehabilitation facility.

Analytic Approach

In our analysis we examined the three key devices used by the disability magazines to portray the men and their stories as heroic: photographs, headlines, and the biographical stories. Photographs of the men with accompanying headlines provide vivid portraits of heroic masculinity. Each constructs a compelling portrait of heroic recovery from SCI through minimizing physical difference and emphasizing physical prowess.

Cover story headlines such as "Campus Comeback", "Moving Mountains", "The Thrill of Victory", "The Drive to Get Back Up", and "No Limits" provide compelling messages of fighting to recover from – and overcome – one's injury. Other stories featured in the magazines have similar headlines; titles such as "On the Move", "The Sky's the Limit", "Persistence Pays Off" or "In the Line of Duty" provide images of men who have fought and won the battle over the limitations associated with their injuries.

The only advertising in *Spinal Column* relates to special events, workshops or services provided by the rehabilitation center. For example one article highlighted the large gym/workout facilities recently built. Other articles regularly feature highlights of the various wheelchair sports events or competitions (e.g. quad rugby, fencing, scuba diving, road racing) sponsored by the center. The advertisements in *New Mobility* are more overtly oriented towards heroic masculinity. The images overwhelmingly portray men's success (or at least effort) in high performance athletics. The men are all young, muscular and involved in sporting pursuits that exemplify physical strength, determination and solitary pursuit of a goal. One wheelchair company had a series of advertisements that featured 'everyday heroes'. Another has a racer wheeling alone down the middle of an isolated street with the headline "Go the distance." A young man is portrayed as if he is entering his first big wheelchair race with the headline "Get out there." A fisherman battles for a fish under the title "Persistence prevails." Another wheelchair company has taken a different approach; perhaps to appeal to young men whose alternative lifestyle reflects a rebellious masculinity, a heavily tattooed, threatening-looking man is shown lifting weights, with the title "Mobility with an attitude." If one considers that these are the predominant images and messages that newly injured men encounter as they themselves are trying to determine where they fit in the able-bodied masculine world, it is clear what a narrow range of options are presented them.

We used Hyden's (1997) concepts of plot, events, character and story to explore the ways that narrative accounts in the magazines were constructed as heroic recovery from SCI. We found the plot, events, and characters in the stories about men with spinal cord injury to be oriented around three themes of heroism: committing to battle, heroic qualities and heroic action. The turn to the hero's path, committing to recovery as a battle, an enemy to be beaten, marked the selection of a distinctively masculine form of activity in the process of rehabilitation, usually participation in adaptive sports. If adaptation occurs when physique is subordinated to other internal values, as previously suggested, it was not apparent in these stories. Instead the embracing of the heroic through physical transcendence was the most appropriate pattern of response according to these reports.

Committing to battle. Committing to battle was represented as the turning-point from the despair that resulted from a spinal cord injury – as something close to death – to the decision to regain one's self, body and life through heroic effort. For example, David had just finished a degree in landscaping and started a full-time job working at a golf-course when he was out at the bar with some friends. Their car took a sharp turn and crashed into a guard rail, breaking David's neck and leaving him a quadriplegic. However, as he lay "motionless in bed" David recollected that he realized "he had no time to feel sorry for himself. Instead he had to get out there and face his new life" (Kisubika 1996, 6-7). Remorse for his loss or sensitivity to his own pain or even an interim state was either not reported by him or not portrayed in the article. By putting aside all emotions he could undertake heroic efforts to enter into the battle over his spinal cord injury.

For other men, it was only when they had reached rock bottom that the turn to the hero's path occurred. Jeff, 27 at the time, had been body surfing when a wave caught him unexpectedly, leaving him paralyzed from the chest down. His high level of activity prior to his accident, made his spinal cord injury difficult to accept. For the first six months after his injury, he didn't care if he lived or died and was still depressed when he was discharged from the rehabilitation center. It was only after a long period of solitude that "Jeff realized he was at a crossroads and decided to be a part of life instead of watching it pass him by" (Sadowsky 1995, 21). It was this decision that propelled Jeff into deciding that "anything a guy can do walking, I can try to do in a chair." Clearly, if a man can't have 'normal' use of his body, at least his efforts to attempt to be as normal as possible makes him acceptable as a man. In both of these examples we can see the way the characters, plot, and story unfold to construct the heroic image of commitment to battle as the first step in assuming a heroic stance towards overcoming their injuries.

Heroic qualities. Each of the stories is replete with descriptions of the heroic qualities that served as these men's primary resource in recovery. Whether a potential was discovered that had previously been untapped or whether they always possessed these qualities was not clear from the vignettes, but images of hard work, persevering in the face of physical pain, not feeling sad or sorry for one's self, and not giving up were regularly invoked by the writers in describing the heroic efforts of these men to recover from SCI. Maintaining a positive attitude, seeing injury as a challenge, being determined, being accepting and having a competitive spirit are the internal qualities that apparently directed these men to live their recovery as heroes. These qualities are commonly associated with extraordinary and thus heroic effort in the face of overwhelming challenge.

A story about Mark, a hardworking computer company manager (Greenhill 1992) portrays him as apparently unfazed by his paralyzing ski accident. He was quoted to say "I look at my injury as a challenge, a minor hurdle. It's almost like a game and I plan to win." Mark's therapist was reported to comment that his attitude was "astonishing" and that with his "will" he will soon water ski and snow ski with adaptive equipment, and play 'quad' rugby. Writer Witter (1995, 18) used racing metaphors to describe Ernest's recovery process. Ernest had been driving cars from the age of 14, racing go-carts, and by the time he was 25 was competing professionally in road races throughout the United States. After his accident, of which he remembers little, Ernest is described as "attacking his rehab with the same vitality he usually reserved for racing, determined that this was one finish line he was going to cross in triumph."

Heroic action. Portrayals of heroic action are used to construct the link between who these men were in the past and who they were becoming. From the emphasis put on this aspect of recovery in the stories in the disability magazines, it is clear that this form of recovery is most highly esteemed, not only as the most important component of the rehabilitation process, but as the primary way to lead one's life as close to normal (i.e., as that of a non-disabled man) as possible. Athletic conquests were represented as the primary way these men could demonstrate competence and control, thus enabling them to minimize the differences between them and their able-bodied counterparts. In addition, physical activities, as extreme or challenging as those done before the injury, formed the basis for a strong sense of continuity with one's past self. Two examples illustrate this point most clearly.

Jim was reported to have described himself as a born athlete: "That's what I was, that's what I did, that's what I lived for" (Dobbs 1996, 50). As a pole vaulter before his injury, Jim became the first in his high school to win a state championship in any sport and was offered a track scholarship to a university. Soon after that offer he was hit by a car while stopped at an intersection, leaving him paralyzed from the lower back down. Jim entered his first wheelchair road race only a year later and went on to become a marathoner and holder of six world records. He says: "I am an *athlete*, not a *wheelchair* athlete" (emphasis in original), thereby distinguishing himself not only from other wheelchair users but even from those who use wheelchairs athletically.

In contrast to that assertion of athletic continuity, another former athlete saw the need for a change in what he did after his injury. Jon had been working for a college basketball team as a chiropractor when, on his way to a practice, the engine on his motorcycle seized as he was going around a curve at 40 mph. He slammed into a utility pole and knew right away he had injured his spinal cord. Jon explained that:

> Basketball and fitness have been part of my life since I can remember, so well-meaning people suggested I go for wheelchair basketball. No way would I settle for less with a sport I had excelled in on my feet. So in the hospital I set my mind on the triathlon. I've always been a competitor and the accident didn't kill that spirit. The triathlon is a grueling event (...) just what I wanted. Two months after the accident I was training 15-20 hours a week. (Jon 1992, 94)

But the 'change' Jon makes is only superficial. Though in a different form, the pattern of renewed athleticism is what is being celebrated here.

Discussion

Reconstructing Masculinities Through Adaptive Sport

While we have laid out a critical stance toward the intense focus on physique and sport at the expense of other aspects of the self following SCI, we also see how physical activity, especially adaptive sport, can be a seductive 'cure' for the crisis of physical disability. Elite athletes with disabilities exemplify what it means to triumph over adversity. Men have reported that wheelchair sports have affirmed their masculinity, provided them with social contacts, prestige, competition, and opportunities to keep fit (Martin et al. 1995; Wheeler et al. 1996). Elite wheelchair athletes have reported the development of a sense of self as "successful, normal, worthwhile, and competitive" (Wheeler et al. 1996, 386). For the athletes in that study, sport aided in "mastering" the physically disabled body, provided opportunities for success, and led others to perceive them – and they to perceive themselves – as normal or even extraordinary (Wheeler et al. 1996, 388). It's been reported that one competitive athlete considered himself analogous to 'Superman.' He said: "When we're in our racing chair it is like putting on a uniform; its like you are out of it now, you are out of the disability. It gives you that. It's like putting a Superman vest on!" (cited in Wheeler et al. 1996, 388)

Because a man's physical strength, competence and attractiveness is so valued in society, many people hold stereotypical beliefs about what it means to acquire a disability and how disabilities will affect activity. In fact, individuals with disabilities may perceive the impact of impairment more negatively than do non-disabled people (Keany & Gluekauf 1993) and thus are drawn to physical activity to challenge these negative stereotypes. It is easy to see how sport, with its sense of comraderie, team-work and shared goals, as well as strong masculine identity affirmation, would serve many young men in the process of constructing personally valued and socially validated identities following spinal cord injury. In spite of its bias towards heroic effort and recovery of physical strength and masculinity, the communal quality of sport may in fact combat the stigmatizing sense of isolation and 'otherness'.

The fears and losses (e.g., related to loss of friendship, identity, and independence) associated with retiring from wheelchair sports parallel those of nondisabled athletes who face the problem of retiring from sport (cf. Brock & Kleiber 1994; Kleiber & Brock 1992; Sparkes 1998), and allude to some of the problems of sport as the primary model for recovery from spinal cord injury. Many of the men in Wheeler et al.'s (1996) study experienced fears about the future, particularly in terms of aging with a disability, coping with their changing body image and losing their independence. This fear was exacerbated in those men who had few interests outside sports and was especially acute for those who were forced to leave their sport. "I'm just like a Joe average disabled person who sits on a couch and doesn't do anything," reported one retired athlete in Wheeler's study (1996, 393). Wheeler et al found that the rapid rise to success for male wheelchair athletes often preceded initial adjustment to disability. For many athletes, retirement from sport led to having to deal for the *first time* with issues of coping with a disability; and this often led to an 'identity crisis.'

While sport may be a positive solution to adjusting to spinal cord injury in the short term, it is problematic for some men initially and for others as time passes. Turning to aggressive, competitive sport provides the opportunity to reassert assumptions about what it means to be a man in making sense of one's present situation. However, these same assumptions also preclude expanding values and subordinating physique values (Wright 1983) and enlarging one's perspectives of life (Vash 1994) that some rehabilitation researchers argue are central to adjustment to disability and transformative change. Our concern is that traditional models of rehabilitation may restrict a fuller exploration of self-values when access to sport and other physical activities that reinforce traditional masculine ideals is so readily available.

The Hero Metaphor in Narrative Reconstruction

People who have experienced a traumatic injury or illness tell stories of their experiences of what it was like to be injured, to be a patient, and to recover. These stories become the 'scripts' by which they "work out their own changing identities, but also guide others who will follow them" (Frank 1995, 17). Charmaz (1994, 276) suggests that the definition that a man has of his disability reflects and simultaneously shapes his life story, a narrative of "knowing self through illness." The ways that men define their situation (i.e. view their disabilities as enemies or allies, intrusive presence or opportunities) serve to 'personify' disability and frame new identifications. Defining one's disability as 'enemy', for example, allows continuity of self, whereby "the narrative framing of the man's definition proclaims that he remains the same though his body and situation have changed" (276).

Narrative reconstruction is the process by which people "attempt to reconstitute and repair ruptures between body, self and world by linking-up and interpreting different aspects of biography in order to realign present and past and self with society" (Williams 1984, 197). In the context of a disabling accident or illness people make sense of their disability experiences through the stories they tell themselves and others. In so doing, they 'become' their stories (Frank 1995). Rewriting one's life story as one of heroic action following spinal cord injury can act to abridge the process of narrative reconstruction. Abridgment occurs when this process is incomplete, cut short or curtailed. With males with SCI, abridgment is most likely to be found in those stories that valorize a particular, in this case hyper- masculine, response that combats the disruption of injury with the earliest possible resumption or adoption of an aggressive, active posture.

The disjuncture between who a man considered himself to be in the past and who he was "supposed to be" in the future is reflected in his stories of disability and recovery in the present. "The past is remembered with such arresting lucidity because it is not experienced as past; the illness experiences that are being told are unassimilated fragments that refuse to become past, haunting the present" (Frank 1995, 60). By embodying heroic action in the battle to recover from spinal cord injury, a man can rewrite his life story in ways that make the present a heroic endeavor and the future a matter of abundant possibility (Carr 1986). From this "a sense of coherence can be restored" (Frank 1995, 61), even though a man's forms of physical expressiveness may have changed dramatically.

Heroic Masculinities as Narrative Scripts for Recovery from Spinal Cord Injury

Illness narratives are not only personal stories; they are particularly influential to our shared cultural understanding of what it means to be ill or disabled. "They (published stories) affect how others tell their stories, creating the social rhetoric of illness" (Frank 1995, 21). Like autobiographies and other testimonials, disability magazines also become primary vehicles for testimony and witness of the good illness story. While we do not know the truth of the stories provided to us in the disability magazines, as hero stories they are good stories that provide a powerful link to what is valued in society.

We took the disability magazines as exemplars of the institution's beliefs about what is most valued in the rehabilitation process. As vehicles of the rehabilitation institution (and disability community) for disseminating these culturally valued messages regarding what it means to be a man and disabled, these magazines play an influential role in socializing men and their families to their new world.

For the men who tell and read the vignettes in the disability magazines, these stories define a range of possible, desirable and socially-valued roles and standards. In doing so, they serve as 'narrative maps' (Pollner & Stein 1996), laying out the script by which men in rehabilitation and wheelchair sports come to understand recovery from SCI as a battle to be won. Pollner and Stein (1996, 201) explained that newcomers at the threshold of entering an unfamiliar social world become socialized to their new world through stories, which they call narrative maps.[4] They believe that these narrative maps serve as 'prepresentations'[5] of reality:

> The maps may contribute to socialization and social reproduction by transmitting the values and norms of the new world to a new generation. The maps may shape action by directing newcomers toward certain areas and activities and away from others and by specifying preparations in the present necessary for effective action in the future. More generally, prepresentations of reality contribute to the very constitution of social worlds.

Not only do the stories in the disability magazines help the new-comer, in this case the newly injured man, understand what to expect in rehabilitation and life afterwards, but they inform him of the 'best' ways to function successfully in these new worlds. As we saw, the primary script in these magazines is one of heroic qualities and heroic action. If, as Bruner (1986) suggests, the versions of the stories we tell affect the persons we become, then following the script of heroic recovery mapped out in disability magazines is likely to be limiting in important ways.

Reconstructing Masculinities: Is There a Place for the Hero in Adjustment to SCI?

If a man garners acceptance (and indeed glorification) and support by being a hero in the eyes of others, and he himself finds comfort in his own hero stories, what is the problem? Our argument has been that taking on the hero's story may bring short term gains, but the ultimate cost to doing so may be a foreclosure on adjustment and self-development. In identifying with the hyper-masculine hero who is physical and forceful in dramatic contrast to the limiting nature of his disability. an individual with SCI loses the opportunity to truly 'see' himself, perhaps for the first time in his life. It is only when the constraints of cultural ideals are transcended, rather than the disability itself, are transcended that the opportunity for personal transformation exists.

Perhaps the schism between the traditional model of masculinity and the opportunities for personal transformation that spinal cord injury may provide can be bridged by asking if there is some way that a man can adopt some aspects of a hero's story, while at the same time recasting the hero in ways that allow for alternate paths to recovery to be taken, and alternate forms of self expression to emerge? Robinson (1995) asks a similar question in his study of men in mid-life. He suggests that dropping the traditional model of masculinity can be as heroic as any other life quest.

Neuropsychologist George Prigatano (1995) makes a case for the utility of the hero's story in recovering from disability. For Prigatano, having patients deal with the problem of *lost normality* was the most central issue of recovery in his work with patients following brain injury. Prigatano believes that it is when people confront what they most want to avoid (that is, accepting the fact that they must live with the results of a permanent disability) that the 'hero's path' is discovered. For him then, it is the hard work of personal development and not recovery of physical power that is heroic. Perhaps the value of the stories in the disability magazines could be enhanced if they put less emphasis on heroic action and more on the heroic qualities of more fully confronting the disability in the first place. In this way a man reconstructs a sense of self he values in spite of his disability and regardless of whether he is physically active or not.

As noted earlier, Gerschick & Miller (1995, 203) found that men with physical disabilities would either rely on or reject dominant conceptions of masculinity. Of the two, these authors argue that the rejection model "offers the most hope for change." The men in their study who reconstructed conceptions of masculinity were all members of the disability rights movement, which defines disability as a sociopolitical construction. Gerschick & Miller (1995, 203-204) described a 'three-pronged' strategy to reconstruct masculinity employed by these men:

> First they focus on changing the frame of reference regarding who defines disability and masculinity, thereby changing the dynamics of social construction of both. Second, they endeavor to help people with disabilities be more self-referent when defining their identities. To do that, a third component must be implemented: support structures, as alternative subcultures, must exist.

It is clear from the stories typically featured in the disability magazines that very few culturally acceptable options exist for men who do not want to, or cannot, live up to traditional masculine ideals. And yet as with all such injuries, these men are faced with reconciling their own personal lives and life stories with a self-body-life-altering disability that is inconsistent with cultural ideals. To suggest otherwise is to trivialize the problem. And when attention is given almost exclusively to the physical forms of self expression the importance of identifying other potentials not dependent upon physical power and strength is undermined.

While individuals are capable of reconstructing their life stories, transforming one's self and life is more than a matter of individual resolve;

to do so often means challenging prevailing norms, ideals, values and prescriptions that shape both individual action and private self-understanding (Rosenwald & Ochberg 1992). When the focus is exclusively on overcoming the 'death' of a former self through the reconstruction of a similar version, a competitively athletic one for example, the heroic journey is incomplete. The demonstration of power provides the antidote to the failed body and the reestablishment of some independence that is so important to masculine identity. And for those who lacked such an identity, the triumph over the adversity of the failed body offers a sense of the heroic that may have been missing prior to the injury. But the more complete journey involves a rather radical 'restorying' (cf. Brock & Kleiber 1994), where there is a fuller transformation and the self is virtually reborn. The *most* heroic moral quest, arguably, is to see the experience as an opportunity for the re-creation of self. It is very common among those who experience such injuries or illnesses to think of themselves as 'better' for the experience. This improved identity frequently includes aspects of self that are discovered as different or discontinuous from the pre-injury self. It also often includes an expanded commitment to others, whether members of one's own family or community or those who have experienced a similar fate.

We discussed earlier that, as narrative maps, the stories of struggle and triumph featured in the disability magazines do chart the way to enter the worlds of rehabilitation and disability and may in fact serve as sources of inspiration for others who wonder what they too face in their own recovery process. However, to the extent that these magazines and stories cultivate a traditional model of masculinity, they may hinder the transformative potential of disability. Portraying recovery as aligning one's actions with those of the physically heroic not only creates an unrealistic ideal that most individuals cannot live up to, it also directs the course of recovery in personally limiting ways.

Heroic lives may not be for everyone, but the advent of life-disrupting adversity suggests the possibility of a wake-up call. Many people felled by catastrophes manage to rebound and go on to achieve outstanding success in the pursuit of happiness. They do this through two primary categories of action: reframing their attitudes about adversity and enlarging their perspectives of life itself. Whatever must happen with life exigencies, these inner changes seem crucial. (Vash 1994, 201)

Notes

[1] Our frame of reference is shaped around the experience of American men who have incurred a spinal cord injury.

[2] This distinction was captured by an elite wheelchair athlete who contrasted his athleticism with others who turn to legitimized sports participation after their injuries. "... they weren't really athletes; they were heroin addicts that fell off cliffs and through their rehab process discovered wheelchair sports. All of a sudden they were winning gold medals, but they weren't born athletes the way I was. That's what I was, that's what I did, that's what I lived for." In his comment on his distinctiveness, he illustrates the exception rather than the rule.

[3] For Robinson (1995) the 'compulsive warrior' model is pervasively inbred in American culture.

[4] Pollner and Stein (1996) studied the social worlds of Alcoholics Anonymous. We are interested here in the community of those with spinal cord injury, or even the rehabilitation community more generally, and the way that people become socialized to these environments. Mishler (1984) provides a very useful account of this medical world for people who must learn to become patients. Frank (1995) provides an equally excellent discussion of the ways in which people reclaim and rewrite their own stories following illness.

[5] (i.e., they provide information before people have actually entered these new worlds)

References

Brock, S. & Kleiber, D. A. (1994) Narratives in Medicine: The stories of elite college athletes' career-ending injuries. *Qualitative Health Research* (4), 4, 411-430.

Bruner, J. S. (1986) *Actual minds, possible worlds.* Cambridge, MA: Harvard University Press.

Carr, D. (1986) *Time, narrative, and history.* Bloomington: Indiana University Press.

Charmaz, K. (1994) Identity dilemmas of chronically ill men. *The Sociological Quarterly* (35),2, 269-288.

Cornwall, A. & Lindisfarne, N. (1994) Dislocating masculinity: Gender, power and anthropology. In: A. Cornwall & N. Lindisfarne (Eds.) *Dislocating masculinity: Comparative ethnographies.* London: Routledge.

Dobbs, J. (1996) Jim Knaub: Athletic, aesthete, archetype. *New Mobility* (7), 50-51.

Frank, A. W. (1995) *The wounded storyteller: Body, illness, and ethics.* Chicago, II: The University of Chicago Press.

Gerschick, T. J. & Miller, A. S. (1995) Coming to terms: Masculinity and physical disability. In: D. Sabo & D.F. Gordon (Eds.) *Men's health and illness: Gender, power, and the body.* Thousand Oaks, CA: Sage.

Greenhill, J. (1992) Mark Phillips: Making the hill. *Spinal Column* (50), 10-11.

Hawkins, A. H. (1993) *Reconstructing illness: Studies in pathography.* West Lafayette, IN: Purdue University Press.

Hyden, L C. (1997) The institutional narrative as drama. In: B. Gunnarsson, P. Linell, & B. Norberg (Eds.) *The construction of professional discourse.* London: Longman.

"Jon" (1992) untitled. *New Mobility,* (3), 94.

Keany, K. C. M-H. & Gluekauf, R. L. (1993) Disability and value change: An overview and reanalysis of acceptance of loss theory. *Rehabilitation Psychology* (38), 3, 199-210.

Kewman, D. G. & Tate, D. G. (1998) Suicide in SCI: A psychological autopsy. *Rehabilitation Psychology* (43),2, 143-151.

Kimmel, M. S. (1987) The contemporary crisis of masculinity in historical perspective. In: H. Brod (Ed.) *The making of masculinities.* Boston: Allen Unwin.

Kimmel, M. S. & Messner, M. (Eds.). (1993) *Men's lives.* New York: Macmillan.

Kinney, W. & Coyle, C. (1989). *Predictors of quality of life among physically disabled adults.* Philadelphia: Temple University.

Kisubika, A. N. (1996). Meet wheelchair boy. *Spinal Column,* (54), 6-7.

Kleiber, D. A. & Brock, S. C. (1992) The effect of career-ending injuries on the subsequent well-being of elite athletes. *Sociology of Sport Journal.* (9), 70-75.

Mac an Ghaill, M. (Ed.) (1996) *Understanding masculinities: Social relations and cultural arenas.* Buckingham: Open University Press.

Maddox, S. (1996) Christopher Reeve: Making sense out of chaos. *New Mobility* (7), 35, 58-64; 104-105.

Martin, J. J. Mushett, C. & Smith, K. L (1995) Athletic identity and sport orientation of elite athletes with disabilities. *Adapted Physical Activity Quarterly* (12), 113-123.

National Spinal Cord Injury Statistical Center (1996) *Spinal cord injury statistics.*

Pollner, M. & Stein, J. (1996). Narrative mapping of social worlds: The voice of experience in Alcoholics Anonymous. *Symbolic Interaction* (19),3, 203-223.

Prigatano, G. P. (1995) 1994 Sheldon Berrol, MD, Senior Lectureship: The problem of lost normality after brain injury. *Journal of Head Trauma Rehabilitation* (10),3, 87-95.

Robinson, J. (1995) *Death of a hero, birth of the soul: Answering the call of midlife.* Sacramento, CA: Tzedakah Publications.

Rosenwald, G. & Ochberg, R. (Eds.) (1992) *Storied lives.* New Haven, CT: Yale University Press.

Sadowsky, D. (1995) The drive to get back up. *Spinal Column* (55), 20-21.

Sparkes, A. C. & Smith, B. (1999) Sport, spinal cord injuries and embodied masculinities. (unpublished manuscript).

Sparkes, A. C. (1998) Athletic identity: An Achilles heel to the survival of the self. *Qualitative Health Research* (8), 644-664.

Vash, C. (1994) *Personality and adversity: Psychospiritual aspects of rehabilitation.* New York: Springer.

Vogel, B. (1995) 110 Percent: The hard times and good fortune of Danny "Magoo" Chandler. *New Mobility* (6),24, 22-23; 60.

Wendell, S. (1989) Toward a feminist theory of disability. *Hypatia* (4),2, 104-124.

Wheeler, G. D., Malone, L. A., Van Vlack, S., Nelson, E. R., & Steadward, R. D. (1996) Retirement from disability sport: A pilot study. *Adapted Physical Activity Quarterly* (31), 382-399.

Williams, G. (1984) The genesis of chronic illness: Narrative reconstruction. *Sociology of Health and Illness* (6), 2, 175-200.

Witter, D. (1995) The sweetness of victory. *Spinal Column* (53), 18-20.

Wright, B. A. (1983) *Physical disability: A psychological approach* (2nd ed.). New York: Harper & Row.

White, P. G., Young, K., & McTeer, W. G. (1995) Sport, masculinity, and the injured body. In: D. Sabo & D.F. Gordon (Eds.) *Men's health and illness: Gender, power, and the body.* Thousand Oaks, CA: Sage.

Jim Denison

MEN'S SELVES AND SPORT

Gift

Mr Davidson hollered, "Runners get set," and raised his right arm skywards, and immediately 31 children – 18 boys and 13 girls – toed a thick white chalk line on the grass. Not at all unlike a small platoon assembling for inspection. Only their heads remained askew, not centred between their shoulders like good conscripts. Their tiny eyes were fixed on Mr Davidson awaiting his final command. When at last he dropped his arm they all dashed.

This was the first time Mr Davidson had his class race over fifty meters. The cold, rainy winter had kept them on the netball courts for PE. Brian Hardy came in grinning five meters clear of the field, which surprised no one. The story about Brian went that he came out of the womb with a ball in his hands. A natural, people said. He'd spend hours by himself hurling a cricket ball in the air and catching it, or chucking a tennis ball against a wall and scooping up the rebound, or kicking a rugby ball and chasing it down. Two kids in Mr Davidson's class were crook the day of the fifty meter race. Brian made appointments to race them later. He beat them with ease as well.

A week earlier Mr Davidson had measured out fifty meters. He pushed a wheel that clicked off each meter. Although the course remained the same year after year, Mr Davidson still liked to remeasure it. The same way he liked to shuffle around the desks and chairs in his classroom each night before returning them to their original arrangement. With his class watching he counted out-loud as the wheel clicked, "One, two, three..." dragging out the final five clicks, "fooorttty-siiix, fooorttty-seeeven..." to make running fifty meters seem more formidable.

Mr Davidson knew how to use his voice. He could vary its pitch and tone depending on the circumstance: deep and sonorous to dispense instructions, full and stern to settle his class down, high and ebullient to acknowledge a job well done, and soft and soothing to lift a fallen player. The way he could play with accents and odd expressions made him a natural storyteller. His body language and timing created such dramatic tension that his students anticipated their daily story hour with almost as much excitement as the final bell.

As it happened, Mr Davidson loved to tell stories about great sportsmen and their exploits. Peter Snell, Edmund Hillary, Richard Hadlee, and lately Peter Blake were a few of the life histories he told. His reports were always a mixture of memory, fact, and imagination. That made for a more interesting story, he believed. He also recounted tales of Burndale past pupils who had represented New Zealand. By his estimate there were five. Two in rugby, and one each in athletics, hockey, and rowing. He never forgot to mention how fast they all were – always the fastest boy in the school, he said.

The fifty meter race started between the big oak behind the netball goals and the hole in the chain-link fence that divided the school property from the Hanson's backyard. It finished across the rugby field by the swings and slides and Jungle Jim's. Seeing as he started the race Mr Davidson could never time the finish. Besides, he believed that young boys and girls should run for fun. Yet to the winner he always managed to give the thumbs-up sign, before later in the day draping his arm around his shoulder and whispering secrets into his ear.

Brian almost lost his title as fastest fourth grader at Burndale Primary the very next day. Sharon Daniels challenged him to a rematch during lunch recess. Half-way, by a pile of rusty hurdles, she was clearly ahead. She attended some special after school gymnastics program. They said she had a gift. A gift that supposedly would earn New Zealand a gold medal one day.

It was obvious by the way Sharon ran that she was a gymnast. Her feet skimmed the ground, she barely lifted her knees, and she clenched her fists and pumped her arms in a stiff, jerky manner. Peter Tanner, Brian's best mate, started the race and judged the finish. When Brian and Sharon were set he stood on the finish line and cupped his hands around his mouth and screamed, GO! He declared Brian the winner. Of course he did. Brian believed he'd won too, but Sharon called them cheaters.

"Admit it," she said, folding her arms across her chest and turning up her nose, "you lost to a girl."

"I leaned," Brian shouted at her. "I beat you because I leaned."

Brian had learned to lean by watching the last Olympics on television. The Americans won gold and silver in the 100 meters. The way they dipped at the finish line to edge their rivals impressed him immensely. He imitated them in every race he ran, no matter how close.

Sharon had no one to back her. Mr Davidson was off on playground duty.

"If Mr Davidson had been here he'd say I won."

"No he wouldn't," Brian and Peter both said, smiling.

The other girls in the class were playing hop-scotch outside the lunchroom.

"Well if Sarah Johnson or Beth Carter had been here they'd tell you I won."

Brian knew she was right. Those two would've lied and proclaimed Sharon the winner. Not because Sharon was their friend, they didn't really know her, no one did, but just to see him lose to a girl.

Monday through Friday, straight after school, Mrs Daniels met Sharon in front of Gibson's shoe repair shop, just across from the steps that led into the school. While she waited, Mrs Daniels would step out of her car and lean against the hood, the heat from the engine warming her backside. Occasionally she struck up a conversation with another mum.

"Nice day today, isn't it?" she'd say.

Or if it was a special day, like Halloween or Pet Day, she'd mention that.

"Don't the children look cute with their pets."

Most days, though, Mrs Daniels kept to herself while she waited for Sharon. She'd consider the various choices she made in her life and how things might have turned out differently. She'd also contemplate the direction her daughter's life seemed to be taking and consider its appropriateness. Her pensive expression would turn to delight, though, when the final bell sounded and piles of boys and girls ran to the playground laughing and flailing their arms in the air as if some invisible hand was tickling them. Sharon always made a beeline to the car and quickly hopped into the backseat. A moment later they'd be on their way. Mrs Daniels racing through town to deliver Sharon by 3:30, Sharon squirming out of her dress and into her leotard.

Selection

Chris fell onto his bed before he could remove his coat and scarf. For the next hour he remained motionless, staring into the corner of his room. Dust balls rebounded off the corner walls, and frail cobwebs stretched across the ceiling like tiny hammocks. Despite all of Chris's attempts to keep his room clean, the dust just reappeared, the mould grew back, and the grime always returned.

Running through Chris's head were the sloppy plays he made that afternoon, especially the punch he threw in the final few minutes – normally he was such a clean player, someone parents told their children to model themselves after. To try and clear his mind Chris shut his eyes and whispered to himself imaginary tales of heroes and their journeys. As a boy his Mum used to put him to sleep by reading him stories. Stories about Kings and Queens and gallant Knights and beautiful Ladies. She believed that her little prince was destined for greatness.

It had to be said that no one got back on defence quicker than Chris, or fed the ball to the man in the open sooner. But lately questions were being raised. Has he lost his confidence? Is he sick? Is some bird messin' with his head? Maybe it's a phase he's in, a temporary blip, something sure to pass? Meanwhile, you have to expect the selectors to make a change. Besides, Taane has been looking so good in practice.

"Gentlemen, you're slacking," Coach McKenzie warned before training. "You're running slow and not concentrating. Saturday's going to be tough. Tougher than last week. To win we can't afford any careless errors."

After practice the only comments Coach McKenzie offered were, "Good work, men. Way to be hard."

As the circle of players broke up guys lagged behind to chat or to get in some extra work. Not Chris, though, he stood alone up to his ankles in the filth of the chewed-up field. He had hoped for a sign from Coach McKenzie tonight, a wink or maybe a nod, something to indicate that his place on the squad was secure. But there had been nothing. Nothing at all. Not a single word. After a minute Chris headed silently off the field with his eyes fixed on the ground. The only sound coming from his feet as he lifted them out of the mud.

Blind Satisfaction

I yelled to my son, "Come on, time to go."

Naturally, he protested. "Can't I stay a little longer? Five more minutes, please?"

"No," I said, rolling up my window. "Get inside, your mother has tea waiting."

Without saying a word, Brendan stomped around the front of the car, yanked open the passenger side door, flung his sports bag into the back, slammed his door shut, and stared out the window towards his friends.

As we were about to exit the school parking lot he quickly rolled down his window and screamed, "Way to go, Brian."

"What happened?" I asked.

After he rolled his window back up, straightened himself out in his seat, and fastened his safety belt, he mumbled something about Brian Hanson scoring a try from midfield.

Brendan didn't say anything else after that. Even when I switched on the national program to catch the six o'clock news he didn't call me "boring" or "old fashioned." Like most teenagers, Brendan preferred loud music with undecipherable lyrics to plain, straight news. Then at a red light in the middle of town, he cleared his throat and leaned gently into the dashboard. "Dad," he said softly, "what was it like to play for New Zealand?"

"What do you mean?" I said, extending my hand to lower the volume on the radio.

He answered straight away. "You've never told me how it felt to run on to the field with the Silver Fern on your chest, and to sing the national anthem in front of all of those people. And Mum never talks about it either."

I didn't know what to say. At first I wanted to tell him that playing rugby for New Zealand was the highlight of my life. How I'd never forget moments like the 1970 test against Australia when we came from behind in the last 5 minutes to beat them. But then the light turned green and I shifted into first gear and remembered 1972, the year I wrecked my left knee in a scrum against England and spent 4 months on crutches, and I wanted to warn him that rugby is a brutal and dangerous game. Ultimately I told him that it was an honour to represent my country and that I was fortunate to have the opportunity. Although I don't think he heard a single word that I said.

A vacant, glassy-eyed look had enveloped Brendan's face. I could see that in his mind he was running onto the field with the Silver Fern on his chest, and singing the national anthem in front of a packed stadium himself. His lips were even mouthing the words – God of Nations at Thy feet... That was when I remembered where it all begins, in your dreams. Everyday growing-up, whether sitting in school, playing a pick-up game, or falling asleep at night you imagine how it would feel to pull on the black jersey. The esteem, the glory, the tradition. You anticipate your father's pride and the honour you'll bestow on your school and your club. You even go as far as to promise God that if he just gives you this one thing you'll never ask for anything else so long as you live.

Brendan didn't ask me another question the rest of the way home. The only sound in the car came from the hushed tones of the radio. *At the end of trading the Dow Jones closed twenty points up while the Nikkei remained unchanged.*

After I pulled into our driveway Brendan hopped out of the car and bounced up the porch steps two at a time. When he shut the front door behind him I raised the volume on the radio and sat back in my seat. With English Premier soccer scores followed by the standings after two days of play at the US Open in the background, I began to reflect on some of the decisions I made as a young man. I thought back to 1964, when I was 15, Brendan's age, and how Danny Murdoch and I used to practice kicking and passing for hours and hours. Then I thought back to 1969, when I was 19 and I had a job with a definite future. I was the youngest ever assistant manager of Stockard's Office Furniture Store. I was sure to be manager one day. Mr Stockard said so himself. Cindy was so proud when I told her what Mr Stockard said. To her, our future seemed secure.

Some days I think quitting Stockard's to devote more time to rugby was a good decision, one I'd make again. The people I met and the places I visited made it all worthwhile. But other days, when all I can remember are the injuries and the losses, the hassles with selectors, and the financial sacrifices, I realise how stupid I was to give up a good job just to play a silly game. But back then I suppose I didn't think it was so silly.

I haven't had a decent job since. In fact, in the last 17 years I've had eight different jobs. From owning my own dairy to driving a taxi to selling real estate. I figured someone would set me up with a good company when I finished playing. Two years as an All Black had to be worth something? But all I've got to show for it are a bum knee and some rusty cups and bowls. That's why Cindy's always changing the subject whenever Brendan asks me about my sporting days. She doesn't want all of his attention and energy going into sport. She expects him to finish school, maybe even get a university degree. I suppose she's right, but still I want to see the boy play sports. He's got so much talent, and he'll learn a lot about himself and other people, too. And there's definitely no feeling in the world better than winning. He just needs to keep his head on straight, not lose perspective. And I'm sure I can help him with that.

When I heard Brendan calling me from the front porch the voice on the radio was predicting mostly fine weather for Saturday followed by morning showers on Sunday.

"Dad, what are you doing?" he screamed. "Aren't you coming inside? Your stew's getting cold."

I rolled down my window to say that I'd be right there. Then I switched off the radio and opened the car door, careful not to put too much weight on my left leg as I stepped out.

Martti Silvennoinen

MY BODY AS A METAPHOR

Three Memories

It is an afternoon in early November in 1997. I am driving my car towards my old home town. I shall be speaking about Fatherhood and Maleness to a general audience. I enter the town driving through the scenes of my childhood, along my home street. It still carries the same name, but apart from a few fixed points that are part of the terrain it has changed drastically. The quarter where I lived as a child is gone; its wooden houses have been replaced with stone ones, its flowering yards with parking spaces. All the same, I know precisely when I am passing what was once my home yard.

I park my car in the centre of the town and walk, in a carefree mood, to a coffee shop to wait for a friend. There is lots of time. I am drinking my second cup of coffee when suddenly I am struck by a bad feeling. It comes as a surprise because on all previous occasions I have been happy to see the town again, with memories full of nostalgia. Why this sudden anguish, strange and even frightening?

Then I feel a jolt in my body. The gate! The gate of the yard of my childhood! That must be it. The outlines of the gate, physically long since gone, begin to take shape in my memory, growing sharper like a photograph floating in the developing fluid. There is a little boy standing by the gate. Waiting for his father to come home.

* * *

It is early autumn in 1979. I am lying beside my colleague Jorma on a nearly deserted beach in Constanta in Rumania. The tourist season is over but Ceausescu is still going strong. We are taking part in a conference, each giving a paper of his own. Stretched out on the warm sand we begin talking about this and that, until our thoughts turn to our own provincial university back in distant Finland. We start pondering the state of our university. As we go on, we begin to speak about our longing for the old *Bildungsuniversität*. In our opinion, the current higher education pedagogics, increasingly dominated by technological perspectives, seems to be more about paying attention to trivial detail than about ensuring deep learning. What will happen to understanding, wonder and doubt? At the same time we begin thinking about whether the university still has any teachers with charisma; teachers whose lectures might actually end in applause. Only a few candidates come to mind.

The sun is shining. It is wonderfully peaceful there on the beach. We go on to discuss our own achievements as researchers and teachers, finally coming to the question of how many publications we have managed to write that anyone could be bothered to read a second time. Jorma cannot come to a conclusion, but I burst out: Three! Some 'profit responsibility'?

* * *

"The jumpers are in the hut warming up – a wooden shack with an iron stove painted red glowing in one corner. In the hut there's a smell of felt socks and woollen mittens. It's an exciting place. You can get close to the jumpers. Hear stories – amazing ones – of jumps, of falling, of trips to competitions, of boozing, of women too.

When the ciggies have been smoked, toes and fingers warmed sufficiently, stories told – then it's time to go! Hearts start to jump. Now we'll see who get to carry whose skis to the top of the tower? One ski each. These are real Norwegians, enormously long and heavy, and they all have Kandahar-bindings and varnished bottoms.

Those 'eagles' whose names appeared in the middle or towards the bottom of the result sheet – in other words our heroes – were those with whom we felt most familiar. Many of the jumpers lived in the

same part of town, some just a few doors away, had a swaggering way of talking and in the evenings headed off in their trendy 'flat hats' (Finnish equivalent of mods?), to hang around on street corners. These were no 'gentleman gymnasts', or fleet-footed sprinters, or slalom enthusiasts in designed gear as 'textile-sportsmen'. This familiarity was largely due to the fact that the jumpers almost without exception did heavy jobs, just like our own fathers. It was not at all surprising that these men escaped the everyday grind by playing as hard as they worked."
(Silvennoinen 1994a)

Breaking Away

In 1987 I wrote the final words to the discussion section of my doctoral dissertation: "Today many researchers in the 'body culture' have put more emphasis on emotions, affective experiences, body image and individual identity, which means that a physical activity can also reflect something else than only a striving for healthy habits, motor skills and physical condition. These new points of view will then also be seen in this field of study." (Silvennoinen 1987, 170)

These concluding words were symptoms of my crisis as a researcher and a teacher. However, similar symptoms had appeared long before my public defense of my dissertation. The talk on the beach was another sign that the needle of the compass was far from steady. There was more 'arrhytmia' as a result of the summer meetings of the Nordic Summer University (NSU) in the early 1980s. For several years the NSU had a group for *kroppskultur* (physical culture) that stirred me again and again. Science began to become joyful. In the meetings of the NSU, sport and physical exercise were approached from stimulating viewpoints. *Sportens tekster* ('Papers on sport') (Henriksen & Olsen 1982) was a little collection of writings where the sports and corporeality were peeled open like an onion; in terms of aesthetics, sense perceptions, historical and political conceptions, myths, advertisements and fictions.

Women's studies had begun to use the slogan personal is political (e.g. Jaggar 1989) or even – personal is scientific (Kosonen 1993). This contention could be seen as a conscious turning away from objectivity to subjectivity, to self-consciousness and self-determination. In women's own discussion groups, memory work, inspired by the German feminist researcher Frigga Haug (1983) was one way of making public, political, that which had been personally hidden or denied.

At first I was simultaneously fascinated by and suspicions of this emphasis on the personal. I was, after all, a man of huge sets of research materials, a real 'survey expert', accustomed to subjecting his questionnaires to all sorts of methods derived from statistical mathematics. Thus, the openness to corporeality, identity, the private, experiential perspectives, autobiographical approaches displayed in women's studies called into question the generalisability, replicability of research – in short, its objectivity.

Among the researchers working at the Faculty of Sport and Health Sciences at the University of Jyväskylä, Ulla Kosonen was the first to write, in 1986, an article about herself; as a sportswoman (Kosonen 1986). Around the same time Arto Tiihonen (e.g. Laitinen & Tiihonen 1990), an undergraduate majoring in sports studies, completed his Master's thesis in a way that differed radically from the discipline's traditional orientation towards the behavioural sciences. I, too, felt that after many uncertain stirrings it was time to strike out in a new direction. I wrote my first autobiographical text about the sporting experiences of my childhood and youth (Silvennoinen 1988) for a collection edited by Esa Sironen, *Uuteen liikuntakulttuuriin* (Towards a new sports culture). In the blurb of his book Sironen anticipated a transformation not only of sports culture but also of sports studies. "Something new is emerging in sport. Its grave face is relaxing and there are calls for more: new forms of sport, experiences, life style." Later, in 1994, the German-Danish social historian Henning Eichberg (1994) wrote about the then emerging 'Finnish school': "In the Finnish research the appearance of a young generation of scholars has caused more conflicts, has bred more psychological introspective inclinations and a more vigorous breaking of conventions in disciplinary discourses."

Methodical Gazes

In an interview (Denison 1998), Professor Norman K. Denzin from the University of Illinois calls for a radical conversion of ethnography and ethnographic writing practices. "He contends that as culture becomes more global, postmodern and multinational, ethnography has the potential of becoming a form of radical democratic social practice. But this can only be achieved, he argues, by social scientists moving closer to the narrative structures found in literature. This could well be called a 'narrative turn' within the social sciences, obliging the scholars to break down the barriers that separate autobiographical writing from what passes as canonical scholarly research." It is nice to realise that this was something that we in Finland had already been doing for a long time.

The three memories recounted above belong to a period extending from the 1950s to the present. The fragments are not in a chronological order but in an arbitrary one. The last experience was recounted first. This is, after all, how memory works: it lives in what has just happened, returns farther and farther back in time, looking in the past for links with the present, even with the future.

In the last few years my mind has been increasingly occupied by reflections on what remains of my childhood and youth. What does my body remember? This is scarcely to be wondered at. Everyone with a reasonably long stretch of life behind them does the same. However, what interests me is the question whether I was, in the past, already the person that I am now. Or am I, in actual fact, using writing to reconstruct myself (Who am I?) into a shape of my own devising, without engaging in a dialogue (Who are you?)?

Why only three memories? Why precisely these three memories? Have I picked them because despite belonging to different times and places they are all 'lucid memories', even if the first memory told above entered my mind as if from behind a curtain; late and from the margins. Might they offer metaphorical materials, a fixed point, of a kind that could be used in an endeavour to build a bridge from the past to the present? Will memory evade language?

My starting point is that my three memories are not copies of what really happened but reconstructions that include both imaginative and factual elements and symbols of social meaning structures (Berger & Luckmann 1967, 15; Brewer 1986, 43; Saarenheimo 1991). The way in which a memory is written into a text (from myself to another) is shaped by the situation of the time of writing, with the result that the act of narration is affected by many cultural and social conventions (Young 1990).

My present status is that of a middle-class, highly educated man with, in terms of years, a considerable career behind me. As a 'normal type' of the scientific community in Finland I should exemplify linear upward mobility symbolised by titles of offices, positions of trust, memberships, medals. I might be a man with my childhood behind me, a mature and settled-down adult whose passions have been replaced by cool rationality. But that is just what I am not!

Of course I know that it is futile to search fragmentary memories for a stable personality, even by resorting to 'language games'. Nevertheless, memories are an important element of an individual's 'identity work' (see Ziehe 1991, 151), an entity where narration and self-reflection count for more than structured indicators of the self. In its talk and writings the self is narrating, in tests and questionnaires merely reacting. Dan McAdams (1985) argues that autobiographical memory is, in fact, what individual identity is all about. Thus, narrated identity involves both a differentiation from other people and the rest of the world, and a new merging into them.

I doubt there is any way of separating identity from corporeality, possibly the only piece of firm ground available to modern humans. Nevertheless, as is pointed out by Kimmo Jokinen (1993), "it is probably useless to offer any ready-made packages of theories of the body or embodiments of theory while – on the other hand – no amount of textual playfulness can sweep the body aside. There is always more involved than a game of mere textualised and thoroughly dispersed subjects, of total heterogeneity and pure attributors of meaning."

I have wanted to write about my corporeality using metaphors. What might embodied metaphors be like? According to George Lakoff (1993, 203), metaphors are a matter not only of language or figures of speech, but of restructurings of human thinking and action as a whole through what may be the most mundane of things. Time, space and change are always, in some way, metaphorically charged and interpreted. What may become interesting are the contrasts between metaphors, that is, how and why unknown things are made familiar and familiar things unknown, how some features of certain experiences are emphasises and others played down.

Might metaphors be thickenings carrying meanings that maintain and foster identity, that lie dormant in some 'body memory' and emerge or take shape through active memory work, with the result that experiences that have been shunted to the margins may come out and take their place alongside well-remembered things?[1] I am particularly fascinated by the idea that bodily metaphors might have the very important function of opening the knots of childhood to serve as structures of the adult mind (Bardy 1996, 152); by giving the self a voice and by actualising the lived body (Helén 1993).

Reconstructions

The boy standing at the gate. What about it? Just before the visit to my home town I had finished, together with two colleagues, a book about young boys' and girls' relationships with their fathers linked with sport and physical exercise. The book included also my own story about my father; a story about myself as the son of my father and as the father to my sons (Silvennoinen, Tiihonen & Innanen 1997). At the same time, I was writing my father once more visible. As I was putting my memories down, the longed-for father of my childhood, who was often away, gained new characteristics, simultaneously providing support for features of my masculinity that had often been ignored – sensitivity and humility. The boy longing for his father has been etched deep under my 'skin'. It is my reverse side.

As an young adult I was anything but humble. Almost immediately after the mild conversation on the beach Jorma suddenly died. At the time he may have been the closest of my colleagues. As young graduate students and radical leftists in the early 1970s, we had written, in the local student newspaper, fairly critically about our own faculty, managing, in the process, to step on some big toes. Our pieces were so full of the most exquisite zeal and the fiercest of idealism that they may have been what made the professor of our major subject to shout to our face: "Either you two are leaving or I am!"

I think that our 'Rumanian picnic' symbolises a turning point, a rite of passage, that Jorma never had time to complete. The future lay far ahead, but what had already been lived through required its own symbols. The 1970s was for me very much a time of a rebellion against my father, against everything that his ideas represented. Even though my father belonged, by the yardstick of his then economic and social position, to the working class, he hated Russians and communists. He had left his own home in the part of Finland handed over to the Soviet Union after the country's two wars with it, and there were scars.

If the boy standing at the gate and the moment on the beach were flashes of memory, the ski jumpers are as if a long unbroken thread running through my body. I believe that my identification with them and with their masculinity is linked with a shared social context and local mentality: with the 'mimetic stage' (e.g. Stallybrass & White 1986) of a working-class, sweaty, unsublime, rebellious and grotesque corporeality.

Post-war life in my home town in the 1940s was characterised, as was the rest of Finland, by want, diligence, dominance of work, men as the absent breadwinners of their families, mothers as the source of security who exerted a nearly hegemonic emotional dominance over their children.

"What might our boy-culture mean? There was always someone among us boys who had to be outdone or something which had to be performed better than the others. We held our breath, shoved buns into our mouths, vied to see who could piss the furthest, compared willies and bicepses, buried ourselves in a snow drift, stubbed cigarettes out on the back of a hand, made bets about just everything. In Caillois' terms (Caillois 1961, 36) it was more a question of rough and vulgar 'paidia' than 'ludus' – in a wider sense more a question of the pre-modern than the modern" (Silvennoinen 1994b).

"It was an 'ethos of getting by' among small boys, a struggle between an yearning for tenderness on the one hand and a masculinity witnessed with our own eyes on the other. I think that a world experienced in this way could not but guide me and my friends towards a psychoculture of a kind that could be characterised as a culture of *uncertainty* – a culture of *heterogenuous sameness* – a culture of *mutual alliance of lone children.*" (Silvennoinen 1993, 1994b, 1996)

In the 1950s Kuopio, a small town in Inner Finland, whose vulgar dialect was despised particularly in Southern Finland, could nevertheless pride itself on the biggest jumping hill in the Nordic countries! The enormous and marvellously vast jumping hill was a spatial experience that filled us with powerful pleasure. But it was not just a space. It was a place with a name – Puijo, familiar to all Finns.

The building of the primary school was its nearly direct opposite. "Although I looked forward eagerly to going to school – an important rite of initiation for us all -the school itself overwhelmed me for some considerable way. It felt as if the massive stone building sucked me inside it each morning, held me in its grip for a moment only to finally spit me out again in the afternoon. In the cold and dark of winter mornings the illuminated windows of the school seemed to jeer at each timorous figure that approached: Looking forward to seeing you again, just make sure you're not late! (...) And the gymnasium of the primary school dispelled the last remnants of the previous evening's Tarzans, Indians and daredevils flying through the air on skis." (Silvennoinen 1995).

Heikki Peltonen (1996, 196) writes about ski jumpers in Lahti in the 1950s:[2] "A ski jumper is not only a sportsman but also a circus performer. It is thus obvious that he must not be judged by everyday standards. In the mythology of Lahti, ski jumpers are not characterised by or expected to possess such virtues as good manners, moderate drinking habits or trustworthiness."

Markku Koski (1997), a student of popular culture, describes the same sportsmen in this way: "Compared to ski jumpers a skier is a plodder of the old school, no fabulous being, no eagle of jumping hills. He is rarely described by means of poetic animal metaphors, he is just a prosaically strong man or woman. In the 1960s the ski jumpers were the rockers of the time (...) They saw the club as their bunch, an extension of the street gang, other jumpers as members of the band (...) Skiing was tenacious work, ski jumping a continuation, stretching-out, of the daring of childhood and youth – a youth culture – as much as were the james deans and marlon brandos."

I have never liked tea, coffee all the more. I have seen a single obligatory opera in Berlin, in the GDR that was, as a member of a delegation from our department. I fell asleep. Ballet I have sometimes glanced at on TV, never stopping for a closer look. I perceive both art forms as alien on a corporeal level. I still feel a 'rocker bloke', who even in his manner of speaking has, after the political liturgy of his youth, returned to his roots; the language of the street and the yard. No, it does not mean an endless string of curses, but questioning academic vocabulary and rhetoric, particularly when they seem to float on thin air.

Why did I, at university, almost never find a link between reading, the personal, and learning? How could a stint lasting years, correctly carried out but without results worth mentioning, be 'good research'?

In this sense my dissertation is a good subject for self-reflection.

I see my present researcher self as a social scientist who likes his work among people. I am interested in voices and stories of all kinds – endless individual truths – which surprisingly often turn out to be collectively perceived truths. Another thing important to me personally are the ways in which my texts are read and received. Do they arouse in the reader self-perceptions of a kind that might teach them something?

This episodic life story is a written montage where remembering links up with the actual self. The text contains rhetorical and metaphorical links that I have used in an attempt to suggest why my life has gone as it has gone. But has it gone the way I have recounted it? Is there even the minimum of truth required to make the tale hang together? I am not, after all, recalling localisable facts: my record in our home-built jumping hill, the infectious diseases I came down with, the number of children in our quarter in 1952, the floor space of my home and so on. Instead, I present my reader with consciously nuanced emotional states, human portraits, words and possibly even smells.

The memories that I have chosen for presentation are part of an argument to justify grasping the present by means of the past. Understood literally this would be hindsight: my childhood and surroundings have simply made me into what I am now. By contrast, seen in terms of metaphors this approach acquires more subtle, even mysterious meanings – something old is still alive in me.

If I had, exerting my adult will, decided otherwise, would I also have become, irreversibly, an 'other'; a mature and coolly matter-of-fact male researcher? In that case I would certainly have replaced the memories recounted here with others. I do not know what kind of narrative that would have been – or maybe I do know after all: I remember that even as a child I was a prudent, unathletic boy who valued good manners, and who in adulthood broke his ties with the past; with childhood fantasies and with the volatility and bumbling of a few rebellious years in youth. But – had the ski jumpers even then left me in peace?

Now when I am, in conclusion, going to turn really emotional, I can sketch a metaphorical pastoral representing myself:

"An eagle of jumping hills!" A bit of a bohemian. Hides under his exterior a good deal of sensibility. Tends to be shy. And a man who at times recklessly attempts to get out of all that on his own terms. As he takes off, at full pelt, at the end of the ski jump, he is keeping in mind that style is important, too. Falling on his own two feet after a jump fills his body with a warm feeling of well-being. Sometimes his feet do give out, and then he goes down so that the snow swirls up. Nevertheless, despite all such unsteadiness, what is important is not thumping down, year after year, at the line marking the same safe number of metres.

Acknowledgements

My thanks go to Mikko Innanen, Ulla Kosonen and Marjatta Saarnivaara for reading my article and providing such valuable comments and to the translators Michael Freeman, Tony Melville (the earlier articles) and Hannu Hiilos.

Notes

[1] At its simplest memory work may mean setting aside intellectual time and space of a kind that will not emerge at formal meetings, or conferences, but which will, instead, turn into a new kind of dialogue over a cup of coffee, on the veranda of a sauna – or, say, on a beach.

[2] In the 1950s Lahti and its jumping hill were considered 'the Mecca of ski jumping in Finland'. As a perception of locality Lahti meant to the boys of Lahti what Puijo meant to us, with the important difference that the two parties, being 'enemies', utterly refused to see any such similarity.

[3] "We Finns have Matti (Matti Nykänen) – the king of all the jumpers, who was and still is constantly hounded by the media. He has done the same as our own idols a few decades ago – flown through the air on his skis and then disappeared every so often on trips of his own design. Matti has tested and broken the limits of the strict, disciplined sports system. Matti's occasional departures from national responsibility for success have attracted angry criticism, but also motherly sympathy" (Silvennoinen 1994a).

References

Bardy, Marjatta (1996) *Lapsuus ja aikuisuus - kohtauspaikkana Emile* (Childhood and youth – meeting around Emile). Jyväskylä. Stakes. Tutkimuksia 70.

Berger, Peter & Luckmann, Thomas (1967) *The Social Construction of Reality.* NY: Doubleday.

Brewer, William (1986) What Is Autobiographical Memory. In: D. C. Rubin (Ed.) *Autobiographical Memory.* Cambridge: Cambridge University Press, 25-49.

Caillois, Roger (1961) *Man, Play and Games.* NY: The Free Press.

Denison, Jim (1998) An Interview With Norman K. Denzin. *Waikato Journal of Education* 4, 51-54.

Eichberg, Henning (1994) Scandinavian Otherness And Variety. *International Review for the Sociology of Sport* (29) 1, 2.

Haug, Frigga (1983) (Ed.) Frauenformen II. Sexualisierung der Körper (Female forms 2. Sexualization of the body). *Argument Sonderband* 90. West-Berlin.

Helén, Ilpo (1993) Urheilevan ruumiin muisto (The memory of the sporting body). *Nuorisotutkimus* (11)4, 56-58.

Henriksen, Per & Olsen, Per (1982) *Sportens tekster. Helvede i et spejl men fuld av lyst* (Papers on sport. A hell of a game but it's fun). Herning: Systime.

Jaggar, Allison (1989) Love and Knowledge: Emotion in Feminist Epistemology. In: S. Bordo & A. Jaggar (Eds.) *Gender/Body/Knowledge: Feminist Reconstruction of Being and Knowing.* New Brunswick; Rutgers University Press.

Jokinen, Kimmo (1993) Ruumiiden merkit, ruumiiden liike (Bodily signs, bodily movements). *Nuorisotutkimus* (11),4, 1-6.

Kosonen, Ulla (1986) Minun juoksuhistoriani (My running history). *Kulttuurivihkot* (14)5, 15-17.

Kosonen, Ulla (1993) Personal Is Scientific! In: L. Laine (Ed.) *On the Fringes of Sport.* Sankt Augustin: Academia Verlag, 48-56.

Koski, Markku (1997) Designia taivaalla (Design in the sky). In: O. Immonen & J. Mykkänen (Eds.) *Mäkihypyn muoto-oppi ja muita kirjoituksia populaaritaiteista* (The morphology of ski jumping and other writings on popular arts). Saarijärvi: Gummerus, 78-84.

Laitinen, Arja & Tiihonen, Arto (1990) Narratives of Men's Experiences in Sport. *International Review for the Sociology of Sport* (25), 3, 185-200.

Lakoff, George (1993) The Contemporary Theory of Metaphor. In: A. Ortony (Ed.) *Metaphor and Thought.* Cambridge: Cambridge University Press.

McAdams, Dan. P. (1985) *Power, Intimacy and the Life Story. Personological Inquiries into Identity.* Dorsey: The Dorsey Press.

Peltonen, Heikki (1996) Miten minusta tuli minä (How I became me). In: P. Laaksonen & V. Neuvonen (Eds.) *Lahtelaisia – Tottakai. Pojat muistelevat*

1950-luvun Lahtea (Lahti people – naturally. Boys remember Lahti in the 1950s). Helsinki: Edita, 175-198.

Saarenheimo, Marja (1991) Omaelämäkerrallinen muisti ja elämäkerta (Autobiographical memory and autobiography). *Gerontologia* (5),4, 260-269.

Silvennoinen, Martti (1987) *Schoolchildren and Physically Active Interests: The Changes in Interests and in Motives for Physical Exercise Related to Age in Finnish Comprehensive and Upper Secondary Schools.* Studies in Sport, Physical Education and Health 22. Jyväskylä: University of Jyväskylä.

Silvennoinen, Martti (1988) Ruumiinkokeminen ja liikunta (Body-awareness and physical exercise). In: E. Sironen (Ed.) *Uuteen liikuntakulttuuriin* (Towards a new physical culture). Tampere: Vastapaino, 182-191.

Silvennoinen, Martti (1993) A Model for a Man – Tracing a Personal History of Body-Awareness. In: L. Laine (Ed.) *On the Fringes of Sport.* Sankt Augustin: Akademia Verlag, 26-32.

Silvennoinen, Martti (1994a) To Childhood Heroes. *International Review for the Sociology of Sport* (29) 1, 25-30.

Silvennoinen, Martti (1994b) A Return to the Past: Memory Work as a Method of Body Awareness. *Young. Nordic Journal of Youth Research* (2), 4, 36-46.

Silvennoinen, Martti (1995) School Pictures. In: T. Aittola, R. Koikkalainen and E. Sironen (Eds.) *Confronting Strangeness. Towards a Reflexive Modernization of the School.* Jyväskylän yliopisto. Kasvatustieteen laitoksen julkaisuja 5, 70-78.

Silvennoinen, Martti (1996) Localities of Childhood as a History of Mentality and Embodiment. Young. *Nordic Journal of Youth Research* (4),1, 18-29.

Silvennoinen, Martti, Tiihonen, Arto & Innanen, Mikko (1997) (Eds.) *Härkätaistelija kentän reunalla. Kertomuksia isistä, lapsista ja urheilusta* (A bullfighter on the edge of the arena. Stories of fathers, children and sport). Jyväskylä: Jyväskylän yliopiston kirjaston julkaisuyksikkö.

Stallybrass, Peter & White Allon (1986) *The Politics and Poetics of Transgression.* London: Methuen.

Young, Katarine (1990) Narrative Embodiments: Enclaves of the Self in the Realm of Medicine. In: J. Shotter & K. J. Gergen (Eds.) *Texts of Identity.* London: Sage, 152-165.

Ziehe, Thomas (1991) *Uusi nuoriso. Epätavanomaisen oppimisen puolustus* (The new youth. A defence of unorthodox learning) Tampere: Vastapaino.

David Jackson

MY DAUGHTER TEACHES ME HOW TO FLOAT

She wants me to give away my head,
my knowing head that calms away my fears.
My head that anchors me in wavering worlds.

She wants me to ease my stiffly clenching shoulders
and my scrunched up neck, to let me back
of my hair dunk down into water.

I slowly let the pool flood into my ears.
The water seeps over sideburns,
wets the back of my babyish head.

All I can hear is distant, liquid roar –
the echoey plash of an empty swimming pool.
I want to cry out to her and hold my sinking head.

I taught her once to splash around and play.
But now it's my turn to be buoyed up
by her measured, reasoning tone.

I might still drown.
I know she's there but also far away.
My cannonball head can melt
when it learns to trust the waves.

CONTRIBUTORS

DAVID BROWN was born in Honiton (UK) in 1968. After completing BA Ed Hons in Physical Education and French at the University of Exeter, he taught PE in a variety of schools whilst exploring the male bodybuilders – "The Social Meaning of Muscle" – for an Mphil in Education with professor Andrew Sparkes (University of Exeter). David is currently researching the social reproduction of masculinity with professor Evans at the University of Loughborough.

JIM DENISON, PhD, was born in New Rochelle, New York, USA in 1963. Currently he works as a co-director in the Department of Leisure Studies at the University of Waikato, New Zealand. As a lecturer he teaches courses around the psychology of sport. In his high school yearbook during the senior year he wrote: "In becoming a man we each have a different question to answer."

SUSAN L. HUTCHINSON born in 1958 in British Columbia, Canada, is now a doctoral student at the University of Georgia (the Department of Recreation and Leisure Studies). With respect to sports she had some success in track and cross country running as a teenager, but the best 'physical' comes from her own attempts to be 'fiercely independent'. Living on a small island that required cutting her own wood and driving a power boat, and re-roofing the house herself, means somewhat independence. Working as a therapist in rehabilitation with men and women who faced their own injuries has been the impetus for the current dissertation on patient-therapist encounters.

MIKKO INNANEN (born 1971) holds a Master's degree in Social Science (Sociology) from the University of Jyväskylä. He is currently working at the LIKES Research Center for Sport and Health Sciences as a researcher. He is writing his doctoral thesis on concepts of father and mother among Finnish young people and participating as a co-researcher in the international research project Fathers & Sons & Sport.

DAVID JACKSON was born in 1940, in Devon, UK. He taught in secondary English departments for nearly 20 years but is now retired through ill health. David has been involved in men and masculinity issues for 15 years. He is co-founder of Nottingham Agenda, an anti-sexist programme that works with abusive and violent men. David has published widely and he is author of *Unmasking masculinity: A critical autobiography* (London: Routledge, 1990) and *Screaming Men* (Nottingham: 4 Sheets Press, 1998).

DOUGLAS A. KLEIBER, PhD, is Professor and Head of the Department of Recreation and Leisure Studies at the University of Georgia, Athens, USA. He says: "I was a captain of football team, and partly as a result of that experience developed an interest in sport psychology which evolved me into an interest in play and leisure." Douglas has just completed a book entitled *Leisure Experience and Human Movement* (Westview/Basic Books). He has recently entered his 5th decade being 'painfully' aware that his athleticism is mostly behind him, except sailing.

MARTTI SILVENNOINEN, PhD, docent, was born in Kuopio (Finland) 56 years ago. Currently he teaches social theory of the body and qualitative study methods in the Department of Physical Education at the University of Jyväskylä. Since 1996 he has worked together with Andy Sparkes, José Devís Devís, Jim Denison, Arto Tiihonen, Tommi Kotanen and Mikko Innanen in an international study project Fathers & Sons & Sport at the LIKES Research Center for Sport and Health Sciences (Jyväskylä).

BRETT SMITH was born in 1974. Now he is a doctorate candidate in the School of Postgraduate Medicine and Health Sciences at the University of Exeter (UK). His scholarship is centred in the area of body-self relationships, with a specific focus upon identity dilemmas and narrative possibilities. He is extremely grateful to those who have the courage and willingness to share their embodied stories of vulnerability, loss, honour and pain.

ANDREW C. SPARKES, born 1955, is currently Professor of Social Theory in the School of Postgraduate Medicine and Health Sciences in the Department of Exercise and Sport Sciences (University of Exeter, UK). His research interests are eclectic and include: interrupted body projects, identity dilemmas, and the narrative (re)construction of self and the lives and careers of marginalized individuals and groups. These interests are framed by a desire to seek interpretive forms of understanding and an aspiration to represent lived experience using a variety of genres. Andy is the editor of *Research in physical education and sport. Exploring alternative visions* (London: Falmer Press, 1992) and he is currently working on *Telling tales: A qualitative inquiry into sport and physical movement* (Human Kinetics).

Gerald Anthony Sudwell (UK) became the proud father of a baby boy on the 25th March 1971. His son grew up in a small sea-side town in the Southwest until leaving for university at the age of eighteen, where he studied for his Bachelor degree in Sport Sciences and then returned to the Southwest to further his education three years later, successfully gaining his MSc in Exercise and Sport Psychology in 1995 and his PhD in Medical Sciences in 1998. MARK SUDWELL currently lives and works in London as a public relations consultant.

Associate Professor PETER SWAN teaches at the University of Ballarat in a School of Human Movement and Sport Science where he feels increasingly relevant as fewer and fewer students and staff know or care what he actually does. This venerable status is matched by a sense of vulnerability that the chapter in this book may finally expose him to all. He is particularly interested in writing about ordinary peoples experience in physical education and sport. Academically he commenced his education with a Diploma of Physical Education in 1969 from Melbourne University and finally completed an Ed D in 1995 after eight hard years of part time intellectual labour in a B. Ed, M. Ed and doctoral program. At forty nine years of age he is thinking of retiring.

Other SoPhi titles

Devorah Kalekin-Fishman (ed.)
DESIGNS FOR ALIENATION
Exploring Realities and Virtualities

Centering on studies of alienation in varieties of institutional milieus as well as on current theoretical debates, articles in this volume speak to how social institutions concretely frame and foster alienation, legitimating the creation of 'others,' who are disempowered, manipulated, and marginalized. The book presents a 'panoramic' view of how alienation is brought about in different cultures, including the cultures which are generated by computers. In sum, the authors afford readers a multi-faceted report on alienation theory as a tool for analyzing social realities – and burgeoning virtualities.

The book is relevant to the interests of those involved in the social sciences in the widest sense: different branches of sociology (family, education, religion, gender, organizations), political science, anthropology, and social work. It is relevant to psychologists because it deals with topics that touch on problems of identity formation. The material is relevant to the interests of cultural anthropologists and to those of the extensive network of researchers involved in cultural studies – scholars whose footing derives from literature, language, art, and communications. Exploring practical and theoretical implications of alienation, this book will be a welcome aid to the formal and informal study of social problems.

Contributors: Philip Wexler, Sheila Allen, Hedvig Ekerwald, Pirkkoliisa Ahponen, Devorah Kalekin-Fishman, Loek Halman, Anna Mikheyeva, Maria Christina Siqueira de Souza Campos, Helen Ralston, Margaret Abraham, Matthew David, Leena Koski, Veli-Matti Ulvinen, Vessela Misheva, Dagmar Kutsar, and Lauren Langman.

SoPhi, 1998, 368 pages, paperback, ISBN 951-39-0199-8

Sakari Hänninen (ed.)

DISPLACEMENT OF SOCIAL POLICIES

Are we truly living in an antipolitical age? Has another exercise of rule displaced social policy? If so, what kind of displacement? Can we still count on the entitlement promises of social citizenship? What is the role of neoconservative offensive, the culture war, in the efforts to question and limit the government? In the name of "what" is this self-limiting demand for government articulated? In the name of Individual? Liberty? Security? Order? Community? Morality? Life?

In this anthology the ongoing governmental transformation is explored not just as a change from old to new but as a manifold process of multiple series of molecular events. In this kind of problem space displacement does not mean replacement but rather a strategic move in the micropolitical language game.

SoPhi, 1998, 259 pages, paperback, ISBN 951-34-0189-0

Synnöve Karvinen, Tarja Pösö & Mirja Satka (eds.)

RECONSTRUCTING
SOCIAL WORK RESEARCH
Finnish methodological adaptations

The 1990s has been a period of rapid change. Finnish social work research has blossomed in a situation where it has been looking for its identity in "the age of uncertainty" and searching for new conditions for its development. It has not settled for ready-made questions and practices, rather it has begun to de- and reconstruct its own subjects of research. It possesses characteristically strong aspirations, which aim at locating the specificity of the profession, its interactive, as well as social and ethical aspects of social work.

This book offers an representative sample of social work research in Finland, which is specifically aimed at an international audience. The book illustrates the development and application of the research methodological solutions and innovations of ten social work researchers. In addition, it includes a chapter analysing the methodological tensions in current research.

SoPhi, 1999, 300 pages, paperback, ISBN 951-39-0449-0

SoPhi

University of Jyväskylä
Juha Virkki
Department of Social Sciences and Philosophy
Box 35 (MaB)
FIN-40351 Jyväskylä, Finland
tel. +358-(0)14-603123, fax +358-(0)14-603101,
e-mail jutavi@dodo.jyu.fi.

Visit SoPhi home page at